WHEELER

LA GUARDIA

NBC

GENERAL HUGH JOHNSON

FLOYD OLSON

FATHER COUGHLIN

AMERICAN MESSIAHS

By

The Unofficial Observer

SIMON AND SCHUSTER

New York

1935

CONTENTS

INTRODUCTION

As the New Deal coalition of conservative Democrats, Progressive Republicans, liberals, independents and political yes-men coasted into its third year of national power, there was a massing of Messiahs and a rupture of microphones without precedent in our political history. For a time it looked as though the New Deal had been stalled between the stubborn diggers-in-of-heels and the impatient tearers-out-of-hairs.

Now it so happens that I have been in constant if skeptical contact with most of the American Messiahs since long before the advent of Roosevelt and the New Deal. I regard them as indispensable irritants, since they supply the motive-power for essential change and because their manifest exaggerations counterbalance the intemperance of those conservatives who regard Roosevelt as a dangerous revolutionary and the gradual reforms of the New Deal as akin to Communism.

The general public has been confused by their appearance at a critical moment, even if it has been amused and excited by their political tumbling and their economic acrobatics. They have now become the most formidably vociferous element in our public life. They are alive, pugnacious, irresponsible and real—they are democracy with all its drawbacks, America with all its naiveté, the men who put not only the "I" but the "mess" in "Messiah."

Here they are: the mavericks, the wild men, the re-

formers, the men with Plans and Formulas, the fellows
who have it in their power—if they can hold their following—to wreck the New Deal, with the very best of inten-
tions. What stands out, in the present crisis in the battle
of opinion, is the fact that all of these Messiahs are of
the blood and bone of America. They may be doctri-
naires, visionaries, mountebanks or plain unvarnished
political opportunists but they resolutely hew to the line
of thought developed by Tom Paine, Tom Jefferson,
Andy Jackson, Abe Lincoln and Bill Bryan, and give
voice to American dreams rather than European night-
mares.

Hence, despite their inconvenience, it is useless to re-
sent them, for they are part of our very selves. There are
plenty of financial Huey Longs in the Wall Street which
denounces the Kingfish, plenty of EPIC practitioners in
the New England villages which shudder at Upton Sinclair, plenty of broadcasters of commercial creeds which
are sisters to Father Coughlin's crusade for social justice
under the diaphragm of the microphone. There is, in
short, something of each of the Messiahs of 1935 in every
adult American whether he acknowledge it or not—for
the true revolution which began with the election of
F.D.R. is a continuous psychological process, and the only
question which confronts us today is whether we are yet
ready to accept the incoherent and contradictory implications of our own ideas when they are voiced by the out-
landish Messiahs whom we still brand as dangerous.

THE UNOFFICIAL OBSERVER

AMERICAN MESSIAHS

THE KINGFISH

THE LEADERS of popular rebellions are so seldom "socially possible" that, by an inverse logic, the shaggy and uncouth is frequently regarded as a proof of popular leadership. Andy Jackson was a crude Tennessee frontiersman and Abe Lincoln was dubbed the "Illinois gorilla" by his political opponents. The greatest single question of American politics, as of 1935, is whether Huey P. Long, the "Kingfish" of Louisiana, is another Jackson or whether he is simply another Tom Heflin or Pitchfork Ben Tillman, an emancipated hill-billy mouthing rabble-rousing slogans or an American statesman.

In support of the former theory—that Long is a vulgar demagogue with more wind than water behind his ballyhooed "Share-Our-Wealth" movement—is the fact that he is incomparably the most blatant, most rowdy and most brutally direct of our popular political bosses. He operates the State of Louisiana from his seat in the Senate at Washington as a one-man government, scorning to conceal the fact of his dictatorship though using the conventional forms of representative government. He has spread his political power into the neighboring States of Mississippi and Arkansas and adopts methods and policies designed to appeal to the underprivileged, po' white (and colored) croppers, tenants and small farmers of the Deep South: good roads, good schools, free higher education, taxation of the rich, moratorium on debts and a redistribution of wealth. Then there is the affair of the Sand's

Point Club, on the fashionable tip of Long Island, where the Kingfish got a black eye; there are his grotesque exploits in green pyjamas, his lurid (and unpicturesque) language, his lust for life in its cruder and more masculine forms, his contemptuous dismissal of any conventional fawning upon the "woman's vote" or cultivation of "the better element."

This is the "Kingfish" as he has been revealed to the readers of American metropolitan newspapers. The group which destroyed Howard Scott and the rage for Technocracy with a little brutal ridicule, has applied the same tactics to Huey Long. Every conceivable prejudice is invoked against him, including the charge that his dictatorial methods identify him with Hitler and Fascism (as though Lenin, Trotsky and Stalin had been democratic reformers who scorned dictatorship as a political mechanism). Ridicule is the most effective of political weapons so long as its object is impressed by it or his followers listen to it. Otherwise, it is simply an uncommonly effective form of advertising a politician and his program—as the world should realize from the example of Hitler.

Against the theory that Huey Long is merely a mountebank should be set the following facts: that he is the best showman in American politics, having used the very character of the opposition to him to win a wider hearing for his proposals; that he is one of the best radio speakers in politics (he is one of the few men allowed to go on the air without preparation—an exception was his broadcast answering General Johnson, which he prepared and read over the microphone, a proceeding which cramped his style sufficiently to make him swear never to do it again); that he is one of the ablest and certainly the most tireless stump-speaker in the country (not a finished orator, he gesticulates, uses every range of humor, is

plausible, picturesque, informal and persuasive); that he
is a superb political organizer, of the stripe of Jim Farley
or Louis McHenry Howe; that he has as much vitality as
any man in America, the quickest mind in the Senate,
and inborn shrewdness; that he is an excellent lawyer, being excelled by no man in his accurate knowledge of
legislative procedure; that he holds majority control in
America of the idea of the capital levy, that well-worn
plank from various radical political platforms for more
than fifty years; and that he is still a young man, of forty-
one, with time on his side, as well as energy and attain-
ments.

It is, in fact, a question whether Huey Long is not the
ablest and strongest single politician in the country today. The machine has been against him—both the general
business machine and the Democratic political machine
and the fact that national politics are rigged against any
Southern politician. Yet, had he performed the same
political miracle in New York, Ohio or Illinois that he
has achieved in Louisiana, there is no doubt that he
would lead one of the two national parties, and would
be enthusiastically accepted by the same Northern "radicals" and "liberals" who now shrink from him as a dangerous "Fascist."

II

Long owes his rise in Louisiana partly to his energy
and his efforts on behalf of the "forgotten man" of the
bayous and cane-brakes, and partly to his skill in splitting
the opposition to his policies. For example, in the primary
campaign for the Governorship of Louisiana in 1928—
nomination being the equivalent of election in that 100%
Democratic State—he failed to get a majority but led so
wide a field that his plurality gave him his first big step-up

in politics. His campaign for the Presidency is based on
the hope that the conservative votes will go to an Eastern
Republican and the middle-of-the-road votes to an Eastern
Democrat, leaving to him the large vote of the "common
people" of the West and South.

At present he is engaged in widening his political base
of operations and in showing that his power is not confined to his own State, and therefore does not rest merely
on practical political manipulation and "dictatorship."
This was proved by his campaign for Hattie Caraway in
Arkansas in 1930. She was one of five candidates in the
Senatorial primary and was expected to run last. Huey
made a one-week campaign for her, speaking six times a
day, and Mrs. Caraway carried the State with an absolute
majority over her four opponents. She overwhelmed them
in every district in which he had spoken and was snowed
under in the districts that he had been unable to visit.

The next point in this program is to defeat Senator
Joseph T. Robinson of Arkansas, Democratic majority
leader, and Senator Pat Harrison of Mississippi, another
of the party's elder statesmen, in 1936. If he can beat
them he will be well on the road to the formation of a
political empire in the lower Mississippi Valley. In a
hasty moment, he also threatened to destroy Senator Jo-
siah Bailey of North Carolina, but that is a side-show
which he may overlook in his operations in 1936.

Nobody knows how the Kingfish will play his cards. His
most logical move is to go through the motions of seeking
the Democratic Presidential nomination in 1936. He may
be content with the Louisiana delegation, which he threw
to Roosevelt in 1932 in return for Roosevelt's permitting
them to be seated in the Chicago Convention. Again, he
may try his luck in an early primary in some such tinder-
box as North Dakota, one of the first on the list of pri-

maries, in hopes of starting a political prairie-fire which, if successful, may spread to other States. Failing nomination, he may withdraw and start a Third Party or he may concentrate on putting a "Share-Our-Wealth" plank in the Democratic platform and reserve his main effort for 1940. As a precaution, he has set the date of the Louisiana primary for next January, so that he can get his own renomination out of the way before the Presidential campaign. If in the meantime the Roosevelt program has brought about a considerable measure of recovery, he may not try for the Presidency but continue his efforts to enlarge his grip on the South. He may even try to get someone else, such as Burt Wheeler of Montana, to run on a Third Party ticket, realizing that Wheeler is less vulnerable than he is and in the belief that he can deliver his own strength to the Wheeler candidacy as successfully as he did to Hattie Caraway. That he desires to consolidate the "left wing" opposition to Roosevelt, rather than promote his own Presidential fortunes at this stage in the game was indicated late in April, when he offered to support Senator Borah for President in 1936, or any member of a "liberal" group whom Borah might select. The "panel" that Huey offered to the veteran objector from Idaho consisted of the Progressive Republican Senators—Norris of Nebraska, Nye and Frazier of North Dakota—and their corresponding Democratic group in the Senate: Wheeler of Montana, Thomas of Oklahoma, and McCarran of Nevada. As an afterthought, the next day the Kingfish added the name of the Progressive Senator Bronson Cutting of New Mexico.

Whatever his course, it is established that Long is a national candidate in his own mind. In preparation for the ordeal, he went on the water-wagon, allegedly at the instance of Father Coughlin, and brought his family back

to the public eye. Senator Borah is said to have suggested
to Huey, in a moment of friendly advice, that he would
go a lot farther if he could make himself a little more "respectable." At any rate, Huey suddenly went on a well-
advertised "second honeymoon" with his wife, and then
sent her to New York, with his daughter, where Mrs.
Long gave an interview describing the Kingfish as a lov-
ing and kindly husband who liked to saw wood for exercise. She also observed that she never talked politics with
him, inferring that it was not woman's place to concern
herself with such masculine preoccupations—a hint of the
line of thought that Long intends to follow with the
woman voters and one which, to the rage of the feminists,
is intensely popular among the mass of women.

Huey's new sobriety has helped him in his public opin-
ions but he is so high-strung emotionally that it is hard
to tell when he has been drinking and when he is cold
sober. Even though no drop of intoxicants has passed his
lips for weeks, he will weave back and forth, mutter out of
the corner of his mouth, and flail his arms about like an
inebriate who has reached the "fighting drunk" stage.
Like Howard Scott of Technocratic fame he can become
intoxicated by whatever he says, yet unlike Scott he is an
intensely able politician and psychologist.

His political methods, as developed in Louisiana, are
the methods of orthodox American politics of the machine school, plus a little gaudy drama. When he takes
personal command of the Louisiana Legislature and of its
committee hearings, shouts down opposition, drives
through bills that nobody has read, and plays the legislators like a pack of cards, he is only doing a little more
openly what many another political boss does more
quietly over his office-telephone. The methods he used to
break the hold of Mayor Walmsley's Democratic political

must be reckoned with by a man who is boldly challenging vested political and business interests—he is constructing a large broadcasting station at Louisiana State University, powerful enough to reach all but the most distant States.

Of all the brazen gall Long has shown in the Senate none was more notable than that which followed soon after his vehement interchanges with Joe Robinson, after the Johnson speech. After an exchange of insults with Robinson, in which Huey scored, the Kingfish nonchalantly strolled past Robinson's desk, suddenly turned and slapped him on the shoulder. Robinson, red with fury, wheeled, to meet a boyish grin. Then, Huey, with a chuckle, continued his tour of the chamber, where, incidentally, he spends a good third of his time circulating around talking to his fellow-Senators. It is interesting to note that most of his time recently has been spent on the Republican side. It was his clever floor management which put over the McCarran "prevailing wages" amendment to the work relief bill, giving the President a sharp, though short, setback, and postponing passage of the $4,880,000,000 measure for two or three weeks. He is a dangerous opponent and the Administration's apparent failure to realize that he is not an isolated phenomenon but is symptomatic of a gathering wave of dissent from the New Deal measures, is the greatest blunder that the White House had made in the last two years. It is probably attributable to Louis Howe's protracted illness, though sectional and social prejudice may also have swayed Howe's judgment.

In fact, Roosevelt's forcing of the fighting against the Kingfish, the delivery of Louisiana patronage to Long's bitter political opponents, the effort to "get" him on his income tax, the undisguised distaste for Huey's personality and methods in loyal Administration circles, after Long's support of Roosevelt at Chicago and his general support of policies for the "forgotten man," provide one of the major dramas of contemporary politics. Whether the New Dealers regard Long as a dangerous and irresponsible megalomaniac, whether the Old Guard Southern Democrats or the conservative business interests have made Huey's head part of the price for their support, or whether F.D.R. simply does not like Long (which would be quite understandable)—the fact remains that the occupant of the White House has voluntarily alienated a powerful supporter of the original announced purposes of the New Deal and has created a dangerous enemy, not only for his policies but for his continuance in national power.

On the other hand, it is quite likely that no amount of cajolery and tender handling would have kept Huey happy and in line with the New Deal. His own ambition was probably too great. If so, Roosevelt was smart in cutting him loose early, as the tactics employed by Huey in galvanizing his hold on Louisiana were nothing that Roosevelt could have afforded to be associated with, no matter how indirectly. And if the National Administration had let Huey have Federal patronage, it would have had to take part of the responsibility for what he has done and is doing.

III

Who is Huey, anyhow?

He says that he is of English, Dutch, Welsh, Irish, Scotch and French forbears.

He was born in the little town of Winnfield, Louisiana, on August 30, 1893, the seventh of nine children produced by a couple of very modest means—the "log cabin" touch. The older six children had been able to go to college but when Huey came along the money just ran out, since when he has maintained a wistful and typically American faith in the value of college education. He began work as a traveling salesman, tacking up signs, distributing cook-books, etc., in New Orleans, at an early age. Then he got a job traveling for a packing company. He says that life on the road was "too easy for him" and frankly admits that he lost his job because he did "not worry as to my expense account or as to the regularity of my work." After knocking around a bit, he turned up in Norman, Oklahoma, where he spent five months studying law at the University of Oklahoma, supporting himself by selling potatoes and other produce for a wholesale distributor. The following summer he got a good job and did not return immediately to college, traveling instead as a salesman through the Southwest and Middle West.

At the age of nineteen, he got married and in the autumn of 1914 entered the Tulane Law School, where he completed the three-year course in less than one year. He was admitted to the Louisiana Bar by special examination of the State Supreme Court, after he had boldly marched in to see the Chief Justice and told him that his funds were exhausted and that he couldn't afford to wait six weeks until the regular bar exams. So, in 1915, at the age of twenty-one, he hung out his shingle at Winnfield and waited for business. He had hard sledding in his home town and soon afterward moved to Shreveport, where his law business began to pick up. The first legal advice he ever gave was in Winnfield, to the proprietor of a small shop, Oscar K. Allen by name, now Governor of Louisiana and the most loyal of Long henchmen.

When the War came along, the Kingfish stayed at

home on the ground that he was married and a notary public. Instead, he entered politics, announcing himself in 1918 as candidate for Railroad Commissioner from the North Louisiana District and being elected. He immediately began to fight for the regulation of pipe lines and for lower telephone rates, lower street-car fares and so forth. The Railroad Commission was converted into the State Public Service Commission, of which he became chairman in 1921. Three years later he ran for the Governorship but was only third in the primary. He carried the country districts—which have remained the source of his strength—but was snowed under in New Orleans. His term on the Public Service Commission expired and the conservative opposition put up a candidate against him, but Long was overwhelmingly reëlected. His political opponents then succeeded in removing him from the chairmanship, but he remained a member. As a result, he was able to devote more time to law practice and, according to his own account, made a lot of money out of large corporations, building a $40,000 home. By 1928 he was ready to run for Governor again and this time came in first among three, although the New Orleans vote was still heavily against him. The State Legislature was controlled by the opposing factions, who tried to impeach him on miscellaneous charges but failed—his real offense being, according to his account, his attempt to tax the big corporations. In 1930, as a result, he strengthened his position by running for the United States Senate on a "good roads" platform and was elected, but remained to serve out another year of his term as Governor and did not come to Washington until 1932, when he had straightened out—or flattened out—the political situation in Louisiana.

As a result of the National Democratic Administration's support of his opponents, he seemed to be slipping badly in 1933 and early 1934, but came back with a wallop, capturing New Orleans and the State Supreme Court, and becoming virtual dictator of a highly centralized and modernized political machine.

In return for the power he had forced the State to give him, he gave the State the results people expect from dictatorships. He has built roads and bridges, a new State Capitol; he has rebuilt and enlarged Louisiana State University, given it a splendid free medical school, while an equally good dental school and an enlarged school of music are in process of construction. He has removed the poll tax by which the Old Guard restricted the ballot among the poor white farmers, and has taxed the corporations, while exempting the holder of property worth $2,000 or less. He has reduced telephone and other utility rates, has provided free school books, has improved the schools and has modernized the care of the insane and crippled. In all this, he had the benefit of taking over an especially smug and backward State—a community which had been run for years by the "aristocracy," a group of gentlemen who tolerated commercialized vice and political corruption, who were subservient to large property interests, and who did nothing—or next to nothing—for the general welfare. This situation enabled him to dramatize comparatively simple issues and achievements.

Yet the situation that he attacked in Louisiana is characteristic of much of the Deep South, whose leaders at Washington correspondingly fear and hate the Kingfish. When Huey turns on his chief enemies in the Senate, Joe Robinson and Pat Harrison, and refers to what he has done for education—particularly for higher education—in Louisiana, and says, "You haven't got anything like that in Mississippi or Arkansas," there is no comeback.

Everybody—including Joe and Pat—knows it is literally true.

Louisiana State University is his greatest pride. When he became Governor it had 1,600 students and a lot of old buildings and lacked a medical school. Some people were unkind enough to suggest that his determination to build up L.S.U. followed Tulane University's rejection of the suggestion that he be given an honorary degree. Since Huey never forgets a slight, this incident may have helped, but his interest in free education marks this explanation as inadequate. In his autobiography, "Every Man a King," Long asserts that students who had completed their pre-medical studies were unable to obtain admission to Tulane, which possessed the only medical school in the State. So, at the end of 1930, he told L.S.U. to go ahead, get an architect and build a medical school. No funds had been appropriated and he was asked, "But where is the money?" "That will be my part of the job," he answered.

He juggled State property around, sold some of the old L.S.U. campus to the State Government for the new Capitol and State office buildings, scraped together $2,150,000, and when that was used up got some more. In the meantime, he built new buildings and dormitories for the State University, a large swimming pool, a stadium, the "Huey P. Long Field House" and other academic appurtenances. The medical school was built in New Orleans and was rated as Class A by the American Medical Association on February 12, 1933. Since Long became Governor in 1928, the enrollment at the State University has increased from 1,600 to about 5,000; the medical school is unique, in that no fees are charged the students; and now a large dental school is on the way.

There have been some ignorant and supercilious snickers at Huey's collegiate antics, his liking to lead the college band (he does it well) and his attempts to function as football coach. Yet this particular device landed Huey on the sporting-page, the one section of journalism which has been inadequately exploited by political propaganda, and has also helped him to organize a specific appeal to youth, by identifying the Kingfish with college life and campus high-jinks. It is interesting to observe that there was no particular row at L.S.U. when the Kingfish cracked down on the editor of the college paper for writing an editorial attacking him. The editor was the nephew of one of his bitterest enemies but Huey admitted to his friends afterward that he made a mistake in paying any attention to the incident. At the time he was just aggrieved to think that anything like that could happen in "his" university, and apparently most of the students and faculty felt the same way about it.

Is free speech suppressed or tampered with at Louisiana State University? No more so than at Columbia University or many other institutions. Open attacks on Huey are unwelcome but other State universities also discourage attacks on all-powerful politicians, and most privately endowed universities do not welcome attacks on all-powerful trustees or benefactors. But Huey is discussed frankly—and criticized frequently—on the campus and in the faculty rooms of L.S.U., where, according to an imposing array of investigators, broad social and economic problems are discussed more freely than in most American universities. An educator of long experience who has taught in a number of State universities recently lectured at Louisiana State. He reported that it was a great relief to be in a university where the existing order of things could be discussed freely without fear of offending powerful financial and business interests and without fear of being denounced as "communistic." (President Hoover's alma mater—Stanford—might look to its own vigilante-mindedness before the conservatives condemn the Kingfish as a suppressor of academic freedom.) The lecturer continued that, compared to Tulane, L.S.U. was a free forum for public discussion of current issues, and that there was more feeling openly expressed for the "underdog," more questioning of existing faiths and institutions, at L.S.U. than at any university with which he had been connected, excepting the University of Wisconsin a generation ago at the height of the first wave of academic liberalism under the elder LaFollette.

Huey's road-building operations in Louisiana have been criticized by automobilists, who report that many of the roads are badly built and that many stretches of good highway are unjoined. It is a fact that in the first spasm of road building, Long deliberately left a good many unjoined stretches partly as a lesson* to districts which had not supported him with sufficient enthusiasm or from which he sought future support, and partly, by habituating the country people to the value of good roads, to stimulate a demand for their completion. In effect he said: "Here is a sample of what I can do. But if you want to do anything more than ride back and forth on this thirty-mile stretch, you'll have to reëlect me." This is, admittedly, a new way of turning public works—traditionally a way of paying off political contractors for past performances—into new votes. It is just such astuteness as this which makes many nice-minded liberals doubt that Huey is "sincere," as our public opinion is under the impression that a man who is in earnest must also be a little stupid.

IV

Notwithstanding his wisdom of the serpent—though he has never laid claim to the innocence of the dove—reasonably impartial observers in Washington and in Louisiana think that Huey has a lot of honest "proletarian" sympathy. It is, however, so entwined with his very human lust for power and his insensate determination to avenge every personal grievance, that it is difficult to gauge its exact quantity.

For example, he frankly admits in his autobiography that his life-long battle against Standard Oil was a grudge fight. Several of the smaller oil companies were among his legal clients in Shreveport, near which oil and gas had been found, and a good many local business men were dreaming of becoming millionaires. Huey was among them and owned an interest in some of these local oil companies. He gives this account:

Several companies in which I was interested were very successful. We finally had a very large concern. Pipe lines were paying $1.55 per barrel for oil and begging for more.

It was just at this time that the big oil companies threatened to begin pipe line embargoes, designed to force out small companies and independent operators.

(Then) all independents were told the pipe lines would take no more of their oil.

I had gone to sleep one night with transactions all ready to be closed for options and equities which meant I might some day be mentioned among the millionaires, to awake in the morning to read that nothing I had was of value, because the three pipe line companies had said so.

At a meeting called by the local Chamber of Commerce the next day, Huey found that Standard Oil was dominating the situation. It was adamant and the little men and independents were forced to the wall.

"You've done this before and got by with it," Huey shouted, "but this time, go do it and see when you hear the last of it."

Standard Oil has not yet heard the last of it. That incident—a very minor and typical incident in the history of any great American corporation—marked the beginning of Long's fight to tax the big oil and gas companies, a fight which has been progressively successful. In the course of the battle, Long carried a measure to have pipe lines declared common carriers all the way up to the United States Supreme Court, pleaded the case himself, and won it. He also carried his Free School Book Law to the Supreme Court, argued it and was sustained. William Howard Taft was reported to have said that Long was the most brilliant lawyer who had appeared before the Court.

Huey makes very little effort to conceal the element of vindictiveness in all that he does or tries to do. His social thinking seems to be purely the result of experience and not unified by any philosophical basis. When he traveled through the Louisiana back country, as a young commercial salesman, he felt the need of good roads. His own struggle to get through law school impressed him with the need for free education—for free living expenses as well as free tuition for young men of talent—a proposal that he has attached as a rider to his original program for a capital levy and a sharing of wealth, by redistribution.

If he knew history and economics as well as he knows American legal practice, he might become one of the intellectual titans of his day, but, outside the field of law, he is an abysmally ignorant man. His political battles have taken the time in which he might have improved his theoretical knowledge. Shortly after he entered the

United States Senate he heard that a prominent Washington correspondent had just written a series of articles which attempted to analyze the current depression in terms of the long swing of capitalism in the United States. Huey hurried to see him and got copies of the articles, following which a significant and rather pathetic conversation took place.

"Have any books been written on this subject?" Long asked.

The correspondent said there had been a good many.

"Name some," said Huey.

The correspondent named five or six that came to his mind, including James Truslow Adams' "Epic of America."

Huey yanked a roll of bills from his pocket, turned to his husky bodyguard and said, "Get those books for me."

A little later the bodyguard returned with an armful of books and the following day a messenger carried them to Long's desk in the Senate. Then, after the manner of Senator Borah, Huey began to dress up his speeches with appropriate quotations from these haphazard authors, interspersed freely with quotations from the Bible. In particular, he seized on Adams' phrase, "the American dream," and has used it pitilessly ever since. In fact, his speech in the Senate, shortly after he acquired his two-foot shelf, was entitled "The Doom of America's Dream."

It is a matter of record that Long's Share-Our-Wealth movement and program for free popular higher education were not born of the depression and cannot be dismissed as the insincere opportunism of an irresponsible demagogue. In "Every Man a King," he quotes a letter which appeared in "The New Orleans Item" on March 1, 1918, contributed by Huey P. Long at the age of twenty-four:

THINKS WEALTH SHOULD BE MORE EVENLY
DISTRIBUTED

THE EDITOR OF THE ITEM:

A conservative estimate is that about sixty-five or seventy percent of the entire wealth of the United States is owned by two percent of the people. Sixty-eight percent of the whole people living in the United States owns but two percent of its wealth. From the years 1890 to 1910, the wealth of this nation trebled, yet the masses owned less in 1910 than they did in 1890 and a greater percent of the people lived in mortgaged and rented homes in 1900 than in 1890, and more lived in rented and mortgaged homes in 1910 than in 1900. Reports from the Committee on Industrial Relations, appointed by the President, showed that wealth is fast concentrating in the hands of the few.

But the greatest cause for industrial unrest is that of education. Authorities on education tell us that eighty out of every one hundred people in the United States never enter high school; 690 out of every thousand never finish the fourth grade in school. Does such a condition give the ordinary man his proper return of the nation's prosperity? What do you think of such a game of life, so brutally and cruelly unfair, with the dice so loaded that the child of today must enter it with only fourteen chances out of a thousand in his favor of getting a college education and with 968 chances against his securing the lucky draw? How can this Nation prosper with the ordinary child having only twenty chances in a thousand of securing the first part of the game?

This is the condition, north, east, south and west; with wealth concentrating, classes becoming defined, there is not the opportunity for Christian uplift and education and cannot be until there is more economic reform. This is the problem that the good people of this country must consider.

HUEY P. LONG.

Long is a demagogue, no doubt, as well as a slick politician, but he has been making the same speech for seventeen years. He can fairly claim to have been consistent in advocating these fundamental issues, which did not become visible to others of our leading statesmen until the depression was biting deep into an unsound economic structure.

His program, as it stands to-day, has been elaborated until it consists of seven points with an educational rider:

1. To limit poverty and share the wealth, so that every family shall own property worth at least $5,000, free of debt.

2. To limit private fortunes to a few million dollars, so as to make this possible.

3. To pay Old Age Pensions of $30 per month to persons over 60 years of age, subject to suitable income, property and labor qualifications.

4. To prevent industrial over-production by limiting hours of work.

5. To balance agricultural production, "according to the laws of God."

6. To care for the war veterans.

7. To support the government by taxation on big fortunes, and to use agricultural surpluses for crop holidays which will support public works.

Educational Rider: The Government to assume the cost of college, professional and vocational education for all students.

This program coincides pretty accurately with the aspirations and interests of the common man and, if accepted as sincere and feasible, is calculated to muster an enormous volume of popular support for the Kingfish. His educational amendment has also aroused the interest of the white-collar groups. Last year 90 per cent of Long's mail consisted of letters written in pencil on rough note paper. Less than 5 per cent was typewritten on printed or engraved letterheads. During the first quarter of 1935, after his national radio broadcasts, the percentage of type-written letters jumped to 27 per cent.

Neither Huey nor anyone else knows whether this new stratum he has tapped represents wavering Roosevelt strength, but, assuming Roosevelt's backing to have come from the middle and professional classes, it presumably does indicate a possible secession from the disappointed "protest votes" of 1932. A large percentage of Long's better-class mail now comes from lawyers, architects, engineers, and school teachers. He attributes this partly to the educational phase of his program, which he recently began to push. His secretaries claim that his followers include two New York millionaires and one wealthy man from Detroit, and that this trio have promised to give him all the financial aid he needs. One of them, according to Long's staff, feels really penitent about owning so much money, while the other two hope to forestall a revolution by adopting Long's capital levy as a road to the redistribution of wealth. After all, Huey's plan allows a man to own up to five million dollars, which is not so trifling a sum.

The Long correspondence comes from every State, Hawaii, Alaska and the Philippines, and his staff asserts that the movement is spreading into Canada, with the organization of seventeen Share-Our-Wealth Clubs in the single province of Ontario, and others scattered from coast to coast. There are now Share-Our-Wealth Clubs in every State of the Union, and Long's files of February 1, 1935, showed a total of 27,431 clubs, while his staff claim to have the names and addresses of 7,682,768 members on file, the number having more than doubled since November, 1934. Long's staff attribute this phenomenal rise in membership to Huey's radio broadcasts in January, February and March of this year. It can be granted that such a membership is essentially hollow and will not hold up under pressure, but merely considered as a mailing-list it is formidable electioneering.

The method of organization is simplicity itself. One reason for the large membership is the lack of dues. If you write to Long on any subject under the sun, he will send you a circular on the Share-Our-Wealth movement. It contains a coupon with spaces for the names and addresses of the officers of a local club. You proceed to fill in the blanks and to add the names and addresses of your members from time to time. This makes you head of a club and you get your Long literature regularly, as fast as it is reprinted from "The Congressional Record" for distribution under the Senator's frank. Each club gets one or more copies of each new piece of Long literature, which the club's president is supposed to circulate among all of his members. The club's officers are also urged to hold regular meetings to spread the gospel. There is a charming irony in this picture of Huey Long making Big Jim Farley, Roosevelt's political Moltke, distribute free for nothing Long's anti-Roosevelt organization mail.

In addition to this, the Long forces have a national publication, "The American Progress," a paper which comes out once a month, the successor to Long's "Louisiana Progress," which ceased publication two years ago. "The American Progress" is published in Louisiana, but is printed in Meridian, Mississippi, the nearest press that has union labor, according to Long's crowd. At any rate, "The Meridian Star" is not anti-Long, as are most of the Louisiana papers, and "The American Progress" claims a paid circulation of over 275,000 copies. There is also an element of irony in Long's using Mississippi—the home of Huey's enemy, Pat Harrison—as a base of journalistic operations against Pat and everything for which Pat stands. As a matter of fact the distribution of Long's Share-Our-Wealth Clubs suggests that his movement is still fundamentally regional. Louisiana naturally contains the largest number of Long clubs; next in numerical importance are Arkansas, Mississippi, California (the "joiner" State), New York (the State with the largest population) and Minnesota (back-log of the Farmer-Labor movement).

As a result of this far-flung campaign Huey's offices on the first floor of the Senate Office Building are the busiest on Capitol Hill. Literature, filing cases, stacks of letters, are piled everywhere. The telephone rings constantly. The ante-room is thronged with big shots and visiting firemen anxious to see the Kingfish. Once a week, on the average, for the last several months, Huey has had to get a new filing case, for letters or for card-indices of his supporters. After Hugh Johnson's vitriolic radio attack on him and Father Coughlin, Long had to increase his stenographic and clerical staff to twenty-one on the day shift and fourteen on the night shift, and his private secretary, Earle J. Christenberry, was brought close to a nervous breakdown. Most of Long's office force, like his bodyguard and special agents, are said to be on the payroll of the State Government of Louisiana or of its various agencies.

A sardonic note was struck in the Long office this winter when two young men, apparently of independent wealth, who said that they were Harvard graduates, turned up in New Orleans and offered their services to the Kingfish, free of charge. They traveled back to the capital with him, but Christenberry, who had heard stories about Hitler and also about Harvard men, gave them the fishy eye and they dropped out of sight. This incident was the origin of a story about Huey's "brain trust." Christenberry, who ranks as an able executive in his own right, claims that he has a "contract" with the Kingfish, under which he has complete control over Huey's secretarial and clerical staff and assumes responsibility for all of Long's business affairs. He is a former New Orleans advertising man, who has handled a good deal of business for Huey and for various business enterprises associated with Long. In its rather Medicean efforts to embarrass the Kingfish, the Federal Government tried to "get" Christenberry for violation of the income tax law, but failed to secure an indictment. It is as hard to convict a Long man in Louisiana as it was to convict a bootlegger in pre-repeal Manhattan.

Friends of the Roosevelt Administration view its "income tax crusade" against Huey with some uneasiness. There is a suggestion of political persecution about it which does not go down too smoothly, even with those to whom the Kingfish is anathema. This Federal drive against Huey and his followers is the most intensive, according to appearances, of any undertaken by the Internal Revenue Bureau, with the possible exception of that against Al Capone and his merry men. So far, the drive has netted eight indictments, two of them against key men in the Long organization: Seymour Weiss, head of the Hotel Roosevelt Corporation in New Orleans and President of the New Orleans Dock Board, and Abe Shushan, a wholesale drygoods merchant who is also President of the Levee Board. Both of these official positions are unpaid. Other indictments have been brought against one pro-Long State Senator and one pro-Long State Representative—uncle and nephew, respectively—and against four contractors, three of whom are brothers. Long's peo-

ple claim that every man in Huey's organization, including those under indictment, has been offered immunity if
he would tell about his transactions with Long. Up to the
end of April, 1935, not one had accepted the offer, although one man had been convicted already.

What is back of this? According to the Long crowd, it
is an attempt to hamstring Huey's campaign-fund operations. They boast that they keep no records of their campaign collections and that all bills have been paid in cash,
for the last six years if not longer. The reason they give
for this practice is that the Louisiana banks are anti-Huey
and that if the Kingfish kept his political funds in the
form of bank-accounts they might be tied up by some sort
of court action. They do not attempt to conceal the fact
that the Long machine levies toll from all employees of
the State Government and from all who have benefited
from the Long régime. Since Louisiana's laws do not require political organizations to render an accounting,
there is less need of concealment of these normal political practices in Louisiana than in most of the other
States. Under these circumstances, it is difficult to dis-
criminate between personal income and the money collected and spent for political purposes.

Is Long a grafter? Obviously such is the inference from
the Government's drive against his income. Yet every
political machine has to maintain itself by money and
gets it by levying on its own rank and file and on individuals and businesses which have benefited from the policies of the machine or hope to do so. It is an old American custom. According to all accounts, the Long machine
levies the usual tolls, although until recently it was cut
off from the lucrative political revenue in New Orleans
and although it cannot expect contributions from the

Standard Oil or some of the other big business interests in the State, except by blackjack methods. It can also be assumed that the Kingfish's outfit contains about as many personal grafters as is customary in well-organized local political machines.

But all this is far from making Long a grafter himself. According to the shrewdest observers, Long has little interest in money except to spend it advancing his political fortunes. His lust is for political power, not for money power or personal luxury. He needed money for his campaigns in Louisiana and his expenses mount every week in his campaign for the Presidency. And certainly Huey doesn't draw much of a line between himself and his Party in Louisiana. Neither does anyone else. He spends money freely, but in response to a question from a fellow-Senator he recently said that his 1934 income was about $25,000—the amount in excess of his Senate salary coming from his work as a lawyer.

The chances are that nobody except Huey and perhaps one or two of his closest henchmen knows how much money comes into his hands, whence it cometh, and whither he bloweth it. The Federal agents who have been going around indicting and trying to indict his friends suspect, of course, that the unreported income that they have found was political money passed on to Huey. He might have a considerable cache, but it would be a mistake to put him in the class of the ordinary run of politicians who are in the game for their own pockets. The Kingfish is gambling for the biggest stake in the country, if not in the world—the Presidency of the United States. If he had been in politics for money, there are plenty of dignified precedents which suggest that an orator of his ability and legal acumen could have made a fortune by representing wealthy corporations. His own brief interlude as a political lawyer in Shreveport showed that he could pile up the shekels as suavely as a Stimson or a Hughes.

V

Such is the man who constitutes the greatest individual challenge to Franklin Delano Roosevelt and to his New Deal policies. No one who senses the acceleration in world affairs or the vitality of the economic and social issues raised by Long would care to prophesy the outcome of his enterprise. Yet there are controlling factors which suggest that the Kingfish, so far as the immediate future is concerned, may be regarded as a constructive factor in our national life and a valuable adjunct to the New Deal.

Irrespective of his possible national operations, he represents an urgent and important force in the life of the Deep South. The Southern social and economic system has been stratified on feudal lines since the Reconstruction period. Corporations have replaced slave-owners and a banking economy has subverted an agrarian civilization. This has led to intolerable conditions of life for wide masses of poor people, to their economic and political disenfranchisement, to race-hatred and to complacent political corruption of the old Anglo-Saxon order, of which England's Parliament before the First Reform Bill gave the world its most splendid example. This system partially redeemed and justified itself by the generally high caliber of Southern statesmanship, but at the cost of a permanently privileged class and one which was permanently suppressed. As a result, the South has lagged behind the North and West, culturally, spiritually, and economically, by at least a generation. In self-preservation, the South must change, not—as the North fondly imagines—into another North, but into another South. Huey Long is incomparably the most powerful explosive that the South has produced for the purpose of blasting away old ideas, old institutions, old leaders and old traditions.

He is, for the first time since Jackson's day, giving a voice to the economic untouchables of the Baptist Belt. He is uniting the poor white farmers, the tenants, the croppers—and even the negroes—behind his program and bids fair to make himself the master of a rejuvenated social system in the Lower Mississippi Valley. This is an important task, not only for the South but also for the North, for, as long as the Solid South is in the grip of the traditionalists and the conservatives, so long will the entire nation go lame in its effort to achieve substantial social progress. And now, in particular, when our world market for cotton is drying up and the perfection of the mechanical cotton-picker is in sight, it is necessary that the South should effect radical changes in its social and economic order if it is to avoid the worst sort of unrest and disorders during the next twenty years.

By aligning the South—or a substantial portion of it —on the side of economic radicalism, Huey Long can counterbalance the pressure of Southern conservatism against the progressive tendencies of Franklin Roosevelt and so make possible a real New Deal.

The opposition to Long, before it works itself out, may also relieve the Northern wing of Roosevelt's Party from the influence of Wall Street. This influence was fought by Wilson and has been fought by Roosevelt, yet it remains a fact that a Democratic Administration at Washington is generally calculated to assist the interests associated with the name of Rockefeller, just as the Republicans are generally useful to the Morgan interests. Long is anti-Standard Oil and it is possible that some of the present Administration's bias against him is due to the pressure of the interests which have traditionally influenced the Northern Democrats. If Long presses the issue boldly enough it may lead to a regrouping of political forces which will make the two major parties representative of something more than the duel between native American industrialists—such as Rockefeller, Ford and Dupont—and international banking interests—such as those represented by the Morgan firm and by the other private bankers of New York City.

There is, on the other hand, considerable doubt expressed by the liberal publications of the North and East as to the quality of Long's radicalism. "The New Republic," for example, points out that after seven years of Huey's control Louisiana still lacks minimum wage and child labor laws, unemployment insurance and old age pensions, although other States possess these intermediate measures of social justice. Moreover, Long has begun to hobnob with Talmadge, the anti-labor Governor of Georgia—though that would be natural, for Talmadge is also fighting Roosevelt. Long has also been extremely cautious about identifying himself with the share-cropper movements in adjoining states, probably because most of the share-croppers don't vote on account of inability to pay the poll tax. Share-croppers won't help Long much to take Arkansas away from Robinson, for example—because they can't. But if Long gets control of Arkansas, he probably will see that the poll tax is abolished, and endeavor to consolidate his position with the help of share-cropper votes. There is also some uneasiness at the Kingfish's quiet efforts to convince Wall Street that he is far less radical than Roosevelt and so deserves the support of Big Business, as well as at the fact that a serious Long candidacy in 1936 would assist in the election of a conservative

Republican to the Presidency. These undeniable facts cast a bar sinister across the Long movement and go far to justify the label of "Fascist" which is applied to it. Yet they can also be fitted into the Long technique of dividing the opposition, and even radicals should not forget that the social and economic cost to conservatives of a really effective counter-revolution is only less than the cost of revolution itself and that the lot of Germans and Italians under Fascism is not markedly inferior to the lot of the Russians under Communism. For it is a final—and sobering—consideration that if you push far enough to the extreme Left you find yourself cheek by jowl with the extreme Right—and vice versa.

All in all, no one knows Huey well enough to predict what he will do. He has done many good things for Louisiana, and in actual concrete achievement can lay claim to being the best Governor the State—and one of the best any southern State—has ever had. At the same time, he acts like the worst sort of megalomaniac: he bawls out his henchmen, including the Governor of Louisiana, in language most men wouldn't use to their dogs; in Louisiana he lives like an emperor—satisfying every whim; he is a strong man —and wants everybody to know it; he has done more than any American in the last three years to make the processes of democracy obviously ridiculous. Yet he continues to grow in power—which again shows that the great masses of people at the bottom look on the processes of government exactly as the big-moneyed crowd have always looked at them—not as desirable in themselves, but as means to the attainment of definite ends. That is why Huey is a serious threat to democracy—because he is showing how feeble the devotion to the machinery of political democracy is in comparison to the demand for economic liberty, equality and security.

But finally, by raising the threat of disruption of national politics and by grasping the indispensable technique for a capital levy, Long may sufficiently alarm the affluent 2 per cent of our people into effecting a real redistribution of national income as an alternative to violent revolution and economic chaos. It is a sad fact—but true—that people do not part with power or privilege, except out of fear of the immediate personal consequences of not making the necessary concessions. The New Deal has been persuasive, suggestive and—above all— even-tempered in its efforts to convince the privileged classes of the desirability of reconstructing our economic system. Long's campaign is calculated to make these same classes realize the necessity of doing so, as an act of self-preservation. It is true that the velvet glove and the iron fist adorn different hands, but the final result may be the same. One thing is certain—that without Long, without Coughlin, without political and social and economic dissent in the air, Roosevelt would find it extremely difficult, if not altogether impossible, to move forward with those orderly changes by which he proposes to attune American life to the fact of plenty. It is the thunder on the left which produces political change; for without that thunder even the most trivial reforms would be labeled as unsound and un-American by the beneficiaries of economic chaos and the heirs of irrational privilege and arbitrary power.

MICROPHONE MESSIAH

FATHER COUGHLIN is the first conspicuous example of Roman Catholic politics on a national scale in the United States.

No large body of American citizens—such as the Catholics—bound together in a common spiritual discipline and responsive to the moral teachings of a single spiritual head, could fail to be a political force, and the American Catholics have been such a force for many generations. To be a political force and to be "in politics" are, however, two entirely different things, and it is worth the effort to understand the tremendous change which has come over the Church in this country since 1928, when the mere fact that a Catholic layman was candidate for the Presidency led to loose and inaccurate charges that the Church had gone into American politics.

The Catholic faith, as a necessary incident to its religious mission, is concerned with creating the sort of social system that is most suited to the mass of humanity. This system has, in the history of the Western World, been the monogamous home and family. As a result of this system of society—itself a revolutionary change from the pagan system it displaced—certain economic and political arrangements proved most convenient: feudalism, the institution of monarchy and the establishment of peasant farming being characteristic. These arrangements worked satisfactorily for more than a thousand years. Since the industrial revolution, however, they have proved inadequate. Democratic governments have displaced or diluted monarchy, and industrial capitalism has ground down the small-scale peasant farmers.

These changes confronted the Catholic Church with a great crisis, extending over nearly four hundred years, producing the Reformation, the Religious Wars, the rise of nationalism, and the development of the Marxian class struggle leading to proletarian dictatorship and the materialistic State. The Church has, in recent times, made two great efforts to readjust itself to the changes in social and economic conditions. The first was Pope Leo XIII's Encyclical *Rerum Novarum,* in 1891, which tried to dissolve the class struggle by the formation of a specifically Catholic labor movement, and with such considerable success that forty years later Leo's successor was able to point out that the Leonine doctrine had gradually penetrated outside of the Catholic world, and thus "Catholic principles of sociology gradually became part of the intellectual heritage of the whole human race."

For finally, faced with the wreckage of the World War, the success of the Bolshevist régime in Russia, and the collapse of capitalism in 1929 in a protracted depression, Pope Pius XI reconsidered the whole social and economic doctrine of the Church and reformulated the appropriate Catholic principles in his great Encyclical *Quadragesimo Anno,* issued on May 15, 1931, the fortieth anniversary of Leo's *Rerum Novarum. Quadragesimo Anno* not only established the principles of ecclesiastical Fascism—that is to say, the balance of interests rather than the system of economic competition, State coördination of class activities instead of the class struggle, and the family wage to workingmen rather than the so-called "economic wage" to men, women or children—but also enjoined upon the Catholic clergy actively to promote these principles in every land, working through carefully selected agents.

In this connection, it is important to remember that the governing system of the Catholic Church tends to induce a political system which corresponds closely to it. Italian Fascism is the most conspicuous example, although Lenin's organization of the Communist State in Russia was based on direct borrowings from Roman methods of rule. These methods include a commonly accepted body of doctrine, a hierarchy—chosen from the ranks of the faithful—on the basis of loyalty and achievement—to administer the doctrine, and an elected life-long monarch. Such a system creates union and discipline and permits long-range policies to be developed over the generations.

The Church's attitude toward America, moreover, is not dissimilar to the British attitude toward its Indian Army. It regards America as a place where the Church can afford to make bold experiments. On this account, the Church favored the election of Roosevelt, and was—and is —prepared to place its vast property in this country behind a real social reform, along the lines indicated by Catholic morality. For this reason, the Church was friendly toward Technocracy until it discovered the intense materialism and dogmatic atheism of the original Technocrats. For this reason, also, the Church is supporting—and will support—the New Deal, so long as it moves forward in the direction of preserving the social order and the social values.

And for this reason—much to the surprise and embarrassment of some of the more conservative members of the Catholic hierarchy in this country—the Church not only tolerates but also encourages the dissemination of Catholic politics by the radio eloquence of Father Coughlin of the Shrine of the Little Flower, at Detroit, Michigan. For Coughlin, despite certain aberrations in the monetary field and a distressing tendency to identify the Jews with the international bankers, is preaching nothing which cannot be traced back directly to Pius XI's *Quadragesimo Anno* and his subsequent utterances on the subject of the madhouse economics of contemporary capitalism.

Yet this is not to say that the Church will permit Father Coughlin to become another Savonarola. Rome has a very wise distaste for enthusiasts and is not inclined to encourage ecclesiastical politicians. The Holy See did one of the neatest jobs on record when it folded up Don Sturzo, the Italian priest who had organized the *Partito Popolare* in the pre-Fascist days. Similarly, the Vatican has not hesitated to leave the Catholic monarchs of Spain and Austria to their fate, and even to permit the suppression of the German Catholic Party, when confronted with political developments which rendered them superfluous or their position untenable. Therefore, those who see in Coughlin's radio crusade a threat of Catholic government in America go far astray. What the Church wants is the triumph of the Catholic principles of social justice, and the spread of Catholic morality, rather than the triumph of Catholic or ecclesiastical politicians.

II

Who is Father Coughlin, anyhow? Where did he come from? How did he get that way? What does he want?

The first two questions are easily answered. He was born in Hamilton, Ontario, on October 25, 1891, the son of an Irish-American from Indiana. Coughlin's great-grandfather, Patrick, worked on the pick-and-shovel gang which dug the Erie Canal. His grandfather, Daniel, was a carpenter in Buffalo, and his father, Thomas, became a stoker on the Great Lakes steamers. The father was taken ill with typhoid fever and cared for by friends at St. Catharine's, Ontario. When he recovered, he decided to stay ashore and got a job as sexton at St. Mary's Cathedral in Hamilton, where he married a local seamstress, the daughter of a recent Irish immigrant, thus making Father Coughlin a hundred per cent Irish in blood.

Now the Roman Church has always been somewhat embarrassed by and suspicious of the religious zeal of the Irish clergy. This is because centuries of experience have taught the Vatican that enthusiasm is best confined to the laity and that when enthusiasts enter the hierarchy they are capable of producing not only Saints and Martyrs—which is very gratifying—but also a great deal of trouble. The Coughlin family was thoroughly Irish in its religious zeal and young Charles Edward was trained for the priesthood from the beginning.

He went to parochial school in Hamilton and then to St. Michael's College. This was followed by a brilliant course of studies at Toronto University, where he took a Ph.D. at the age of twenty. He went abroad for a few months and then returned, determined finally to enter the priesthood. He was ordained four years later and was assigned to teach English at Assumption College, Sandwich, Ontario.

In 1921, he began to go to Detroit once a week to preach a sermon at St. Agnes' Church and two years later was definitely assigned to the Detroit Diocese under Bishop Gallagher. After assisting at various Detroit churches, he was sent in 1926 to the little frame mission church in the parish of Royal Oak, about twenty miles from the heart of Detroit, a small cure containing only about twenty Catholic families, mainly Irish workmen. From the start,

Coughlin's forte was his Irish eloquence. Everything else was against him. The parish was weak and impoverished and he had trouble with the Ku Klux Klan, which burned a Fiery Cross beside the little church. Yet he represented an ambitious plan. Bishop Gallagher, who had been to Rome in 1925 for the canonization of St. Theresa of the Little Flower and the Child Jesus (a young nun who had died in 1897), thought it would be a fine thing to build a church in her honor in Royal Oak parish and had selected Coughlin for the job.

Coughlin fell in eagerly with his superior's plan. To help strengthen his parish and raise money for his church, he got the idea of using his gift—a fine voice and a sound Catholic training in Ciceronian rhetoric—in broadcasting a weekly sermon. At first he obtained the use of Station WJR, owned by the Detroit "Free Press." After a time he began to give a series of addresses for children. Then he began to broaden out and talk about current social questions.

This gave him his opportunity. In 1929, two other stations were added to his hook-up, and in 1930, after over three years' practice, he suddenly discovered that he was a "power" over the radio. He promptly organized the Radio League of the Little Flower and engaged time on stations outside Detroit. The response was a steadily increasing volume of letters and contributions. As the depression bit into the bones of America, he found that his talks on social and economic subjects were gaining him fame. By 1932, he was able to engage time on a Columbia hook-up of sixteen stations, later enlarged to twenty-seven. Coughlin, backed by the Encyclical of May 15, 1931, was now a major political force. One attack on Hoover brought him in about 1,200,000 letters. Another broadcast, attacking Morgan, Mellon, Mills and Meyer, brought in about 600,000 letters.

He followed his attacks on the bankers and Republicans by broadcasts against the Communists. Then he took a crack at Prohibition. Gosh! how the money rolled in! He was able to spend $15,000 a week and more for broadcasting time, to pay his huge stenographic force, build a 150-foot Crucifixion Tower and put up a $750,000 shell for his new church.

As his attacks on the bankers became stronger, the Columbia Broadcasting System which, after all, was brought into being by bankers, tried to censor Coughlin or shut down on him. Coughlin promptly raised the issue in his next broadcast, and Columbia was so swamped by protests that it abandoned the attempt to put the screws on the voice of the Little Flower. So the construction work proceeded until the tower was completed and the new stone church was constructed, although it still lacks interior furnishings. Coughlin has his own study in the top floor of the tower, while the lower floors are occupied by the clerical force which handles his mail and tots up the contributions.

The next move of Coughlin's opposition was equally obvious—to try to get him through his ecclesiastical superiors. Three times Cardinal O'Connell, Boston's majestic and Smoot-minded prelate, criticized Coughlin publicly. Each time Coughlin replied that the cardinal, while a high dignitary of the Church, was not his superior officer, and he added to this observation an open accusation that O'Connell was ignoring the social doctrine of the Church, as set forth by Pope Pius XI, whose election by the College of Cardinals O'Connell had hoped to prevent. Coughlin is, in fact, responsible to Bishop Gal-

lagher, who has backed him against all attackers. It was
Gallagher, apparently, who restrained him after General
Johnson's radio attack, with its brutal personalities—
"sanctified shell-game," "political bundling" and such—
and persuaded him to come out again for "Roosevelt."
After all, the Church is backing Roosevelt, even though it
may be urging him on in the policies it desires him to
follow. Gallagher, incidentally, is as Irish as Coughlin and
was one of the leaders of the Irish independence movement in this country until the Church made him withdraw. It is as one United Irishman to another that Coughlin calls Liberty bonds "bloody bonds" and hits at the
international bankers who make London the base of their
financial empire.

Despite the splendor of his Parish Church, Coughlin
lives simply, in a little bungalow near the Church of
the Shrine of the Little Flower. Notwithstanding his
large financial responsibilities, he remains essentially a
preacher. His voice ranges from a low croon, oozing with
emotion, to a clear bell-like ring which recalls William
Jennings Bryan. His style is a blend of biting irony and
well-ordered rhetoric, which makes few concessions to the
popular wise-cracks and the vulgarisms of the Huey Long-
Hugh Johnson school. When he needs vituperation, he
simply digs into the Bible for his epithets and parables—
as do they—but his mastery of the Ciceronian method, particularly of *praeteritio,* that trick which orators employ
when they say, "I shall not mention the fact that your
father was a horse-thief and I disdain to refer to your
recent incarceration for a statutory offense," helps him to
achieve heights of high-toned denunciation where Johnson and Long pant along in the valleys of juvenile abuse
and mere name-calling.

Coughlin looks his part: a round-faced, smooth-faced,

pink-skinned Irishman, with that plump, well-padded look that goes with so many Irish priests. He wears glasses —but they are not rose-tinted.

III

The inventions of Hertz, Marconi and DeForest have enabled him to reach incomparably the widest congregation of any preacher recorded in history. His files contain about five million names and addresses, catalogued according to State and county, from which he hopes to build up his National Union for Social Justice to an active membership of more than five million. In the spring of 1934 he discontinued his broadcasts for a while but started them again in the autumn when he began the organization of his National Union—itself a proceeding strikingly reminiscent of the formation of the post-War Catholic political parties in Europe. The response was so great that he got enough money to keep him at the microphone through the winter and spring.

For Coughlin is now a major political power in North America. With his enormous regular audience—greater than that of any member of his Church in the past or present—and his rapidly growing National Union for Social Justice he is treated with marked respect when he appears before a Congressional committee. He has already influenced national politics, in the campaign of 1932. He visited Roosevelt at Albany in the late summer of 1932 and stalked up and down the study of the gingerbread Governor's Mansion, telling F.D.R. what he should do and say. Part of his advice was to go easy in handling Jimmy Walker, who was on trial before Governor Roosevelt's Commission at that time. Later on, Roosevelt repaid Coughlin by stopping off in Detroit on a Sunday and delivering a sermon on "Social Justice," in which he quoted from the Papal Encyclicals, as well as from Jewish and Protestant creeds and writings. This speech cemented the New Deal-Catholic working alliance.

In return, Coughlin supported the New Deal loyally. In the Michigan banking crisis of February, 1933, which led up to the nation-wide moratorium, he denounced the Detroit bankers unmercifully and urged their prosecution and conviction. His indignation was not allayed by the current rumor that the Detroit crisis was caused by an attempt of the New York bankers to catch Henry Ford's financial reserves and so get into his business. During 1933 and the early part of 1934 he was strong for the New Deal and coined the slogan of "Roosevelt or Ruin," which summarized the popular reaction of the time.

Then Coughlin's interests led him to take up money matters—on which the Great Encyclical was studiously vague—and he began advocating free silver, retirement of the national debt with non-interest-bearing notes, and a central bank. As Roosevelt was chilly toward the silverites, Coughlin began to cool off but in November, 1933, when Al Smith was denouncing Roosevelt's "baloney dollar," Coughlin went to New York and broke the back of the "sound money" crowd and their captive balloon, Al, with his speech at the Hippodrome in support of Roosevelt's gold purchase policy. Coughlin drew 30,000 people while the "sound money" people's meeting on the same night failed to fill Carnegie Hall.

The real break between Coughlin and the New Deal came when Henry Morgenthau published the list of large holders of silver, bringing out the fact that the secretary of Coughlin's Radio League was carrying silver futures to the extent of 500,000 ounces. Coughlin, who had been advocating free silver, appeared to take it calmly and explained that he had consistently urged the purchase of commodities, that he favored an increase in the price level and the remonetization of silver, and that he expected the President to bring them about. He added that the silver bullion didn't belong to him but to his organization and that silver was considered one of the best investments for these funds. He later announced that the investment yielded a profit of $12,000.

At any rate, after this incident Coughlin became distinctly cooler toward the New Deal and, in the fall and early winter of 1934–35, he took a few pokes at Roosevelt and at members of his Administration, and was reported to be rather bitter in private. The next time he visited Washington he was at pains to have a talk with Huey Long, after which the Long people said that Coughlin had promised not to oppose Long in the Presidential primaries of 1936 and had hinted that he might help him. As a result of the dawning realization of the New Dealers that a Long-Coughlin alliance was possible and would be embarrassing, Hugh Johnson felt impelled to deliver his blast at these two "Catilines," in the hope of driving a wedge between Coughlin and conservative Catholic opinion. To do this, Johnson charged that there was an alliance between the two men, when there was only a mild political flirtation. He was successful, in that he had the effect of driving Coughlin back—for the time being, at least—into the Roosevelt camp, much to Huey's disgust.

Coughlin's strength rests on far more than his sugary, sanctimonious voice and his gift for suave rhetoric. It rests on the doctrines of social justice advanced by the liberal Encyclicals of Leo XIII and Pius XI and on the support of Coughlin's superior, the liberal Bishop Gallagher of Detroit. His eloquence is, therefore, only the vehicle for giving effect to a great organization's deliberate social policy.

He has taken the Papal Encyclicals very seriously and has not departed very far from their literal meaning. In fact, his personal familiarity with economic and social problems is, like his political philosophy, pretty much of a grab-bag affair. The trend of his speeches suggests that he was accidental, rather than intentional, in his discovery that his views on contemporary politics were popular. This forced him to talk much faster than he could learn the facts—on one occasion, the publishers of "The Economic Consequences of the New Deal," by Stolberg and Vinton, asserted that he had simply paraphrased whole passages of this document. He had no particular background in economics and it was probably pure chance that some of the money cranks got his ear at an early stage and sold him on their greenback and silver panaceas. The Encyclicals gave him no lead in this field and Coughlin fell for the idea that monetary manipulation was the best short-cut to social justice. He concentrated on money— one of the few important questions of the age on which there has been little or no coherent thinking or doctrine through the course of the last ten centuries—and only began to branch out a little in 1934. Away from the Encyclicals, his thinking has so far been consistently foggy.

When he set out to organize his super-lobby, the five million members of his National Union for Social Justice, he based its sixteen planks pretty squarely on the writings of Pius XI, and added a few monetary revelations of his own:

1. Liberty of conscience and education.

2. "A just and living annual wage," commensurate with American standards of decency, for every citizen willing and able to work.

3. Nationalization of banking credit and currency, power, light, oil and natural gas, and "our God-given natural resources."

4. Private ownership of all other property.

5. Control of privately-owned property for the public good.

6. Substitution of a government-owned Central Bank for the privately-owned Federal Reserve system.

7. Rescue of the right to coin and regulate the value of money from the "hands of private owners."

8. Maintenance by the Central Bank of the cost of living at an even keel and repayment of dollar debts with "equal value dollars."

9. Cost of production plus a "fair profit" for the farmer.

10. Government aid to labor in organizing.

11. Recall of all "non-productive" bonds.

12. Abolition of tax-exempt bonds.

13. "Broadening of the base of taxation founded upon the ownership of wealth and capacity to pay."

14. Simplification of government and further lifting of taxation from the laboring class.

15. Conscription of wealth as well as of men in case of a war of self-defense.

16. The establishment of "human rights" above "property rights."

As a result of this program and of Coughlin's National Union, a good many radicals, liberals and old-fashioned conservatives fear that Coughlin is a "Fascist" and there has arisen a good deal of discussion of "Fascism under the Cross" and religious discipline as a substitute for black shirts and Storm Troopers. In this connection, it is noteworthy that the principles of the N.U.S.J. are silent on the subject of free speech, freedom of the press and upholding the Constitution of the United States. Moreover, in an article written for Ray Moley's "Today," Coughlin was at pains to point out that the American form of government had been unbalanced by Roosevelt's assumption of vast powers and by the activity of the President and his appointees in "initiating laws."

"Call this democracy, if you will," Coughlin wrote, "but it is not the same kind of democracy which was conceived by Jefferson, Washington, and Adams. To put it mildly, it is an evolutionized form of democratic government. Or, to express it harshly, it is a revolution which has silently gone on with little and negligible protest coming from the mass of the American people."

The fact that Father Coughlin is not infallible in his interpretation of political developments was revealed by Congress going native in 1935, which resulted in relegating the notion that Roosevelt was a "dictator" to the ashcan of forgotten epithets. It is important only as showing Coughlin's trend of mind in the light of the *Quadragesimo Anno's* recommendation that, in government, "a graded hierarchical order exist between the various subsidiary organizations" and that the State be the arbiter of society "in kingly fashion." Coughlin has asserted on several occasions that if democracy, even in America, is weakening, it is largely because of the "decadence of capitalism." He has also said that what we have called "democracy" has really been "plutocracy." In his article for "Today" he wrote, "By no means do I subscribe to the opinion that, if capitalism is worn out beyond repair, we must then adopt communism, socialism, or even fascism. I simply mean that capitalism has become so identified with abuses which encumber it that its nature is merged with the abuses. Their removal means the burial of capitalism."

In its place, he foresees a "new system based on the belief that wealth is not money, but that wealth is created by the union of capital and labor; and that this wealth must be distributed, even through the intervention of the government, in such a way that every laborer who cooperates in producing this wealth shall have that share of it which will enable him to enjoy, according to his merits, the things that we are capable of growing and of manufacturing as a nation."

This new, if rather vague, technique he calls "social justice," under a system in which private property is identified with a sense of "religious stewardship."

IV

For reasons which will later become obvious, the important question in all this is the extent to which Coughlin's program corresponds with the views of the Vatican. Coughlin is not a clear-cut thinker. He gargles his ideas and is easily carried away by his own stream of oratory.

For example, Coughlin has created considerable apprehension by that plank in his platform which says, "I believe not only in the right of the laboring man to organize in unions but also in the duty of the Government which that laboring man supports to facilitate and to protect these organizations against the vested interests of wealth and intellect."

Does this mean the "corporative state" of Mussolini? And what are "vested interests of intellect"? Some liberals and radicals have been puzzled by that phrase. They ought to be, as the phrase is directed at them, as may be discovered in *Quadragesimo Anno*. Pope Pius XI specifically mentions the "error" of "the 'intellectuals,' as they are called, who set up in opposition . . . another equally false moral principle: that all products and profits, excepting those required to repair and replace invested capital, belong by every right to the workingman. . . . It is an alluring poison, consumed with avidity by many not deceived by open Socialism." Apparently, Coughlin's plank set down his hazy idea of what the Pope meant in this Encyclical. Pius desires to steer a middle and just course—a little to the left of center?—between the "vested interests of wealth" who want to squeeze the income of labor down to the lowest possible point at which labor will function and the "vested interests of intellect" who would deny capital any profit, and specifically refers to the two extremes as the "Unjust Claims of Capital" and the "Unjust Claims of Labor."

It is, on the other hand, both true and natural that the Encyclical should say some pleasant things about the corporative state, forbidding strikes and lockouts by public authority, and leading to "peaceful collaboration of the classes, repression of Socialist organizations and efforts, the moderating influence of a special ministry." Yet the Pope expressed misgivings as to the "excessively bureaucratic and political character" of such a state and suggested that the *sine qua non* of any better social order was "the coöperation of all men of good will."

The natural tendency of the Church is Fascist—that is to say, it relies on the authoritarian principle, on discipline, doctrine administered through a hierarchy—and its policy is inflexibly anti-Communist. But that does not mean that the Church is Fascist, as Americans commonly misunderstand the meaning of the word. The doctrine is the thing—social justice according to a particular idea of what social justice should be—and the mechanism suggests itself once the goal is agreed upon. To obtain justice, the Pope recommends the socialization of certain types of property:

"For it is rightly contended that certain forms of property must be reserved to the State, since they carry with them an opportunity of domination too great to be left to private individuals without injury to the community at large."

This is Coughlin's justification for his demand that we nationalize banks, natural resources and so on.

The real weakness of Coughlin's position is the danger that he fail to realize that his importance is due to the Church which gave him the doctrines that he utters and whose organization not only trained him but provided him with a microphone. His financial and political success has given him an air of sanctified omniscience that sits uneasily on the stomachs of those who deal with him. In 1934, when he testified on the money question before a Congressional Committee, he drove some of the Committee members and some of the public half mad, but his ecclesiastical position prevented them from giving vent to their feelings. On this occasion he gave the impression that he was speaking by divine inspiration on the subject of money, until the only appropriate expression after every question was "Gangway fo' de Lawd Gawd Jehovah!" Each question produced, not an answer, but a long speech and in the end he left the stand, having cast pearls of honeyed eloquence before Congressional inflationists, but having only infected them with a desire to rush down a steep place into the sea. When he broadcasts, of course, he is well supplied with facts and figures, but his general line is pretty hazy.

The conservative wing of the Catholic Church is unduly alarmed over him. Liberal clerics of greater erudition than Coughlin probably have misgivings but they say that, after all, he is preaching the doctrine of the great liberal Encyclicals, which many of the Catholic bishops conspicuously ignore. The great liberal Catholic scholar, Monsignor John A. Ryan, also interprets the Encyclicals in American terms, much as Coughlin does, but with greater learning, tolerance and moderation. And it is probable that his efforts have far more effect on the social thinking of the New Deal than does the rabble-rousing method of the radio priest.

Some people see an anti-Jewish tinge in Coughlin's attack on the international bankers. In his reply to Johnson, he mentioned Baruch, Kuhn, Loeb & Co., the Warburgs and the Rothschilds, and some New York rabbis rose to accuse him of fomenting racial hatred. But in his speech he also mentioned the Morgans, so the anti-Semitic interpretation is still pretty far-fetched, although it should be noted that the Roman Church has never pretended to be pro-Jewish.

Of greater interest to his superiors is the fact that Coughlin commands a wide Protestant following, especially in the Farm Belt, in addition to his Catholic supporters. A good many of his planks appear in the platform of the Farmer-Labor Party—as they do in other liberal platforms—but his plank to give cost of production to the farmer fits in precisely with the radical farm groups, from Milo Reno's Farm Holiday crowd to the Farmer-Labor gang, and two or three of the Farmer-Labor leaders have openly mentioned Coughlin as the leading candidate for President on a Third Party ticket. As he was born in Canada—though of an American father—Coughlin is presumably ineligible for the Presidency under the Constitution, if the Constitution is going to count for anything in the future, and so far as is known, Coughlin's father did not bother to assert his American citizenship after his emigration to Canada and did not register young Charles E.'s birth with an American Consul.

Yet Coughlin's influence is bound to be a big factor in the next Presidential campaign. Anybody who commands so wide an audience and has millions of names on file is automatically a big political force. Long went to see him and others will follow Long. Who can say what thoughts are running through the radio priest's mind? So far he has shown no sign of wishing to leave the Church and, so long as he is in the Church, he will remain under the authority of Bishop Gallagher and, through the Bishop, of his superiors. His most recent statements, of course, have been denials of any intention to form a "Third Party."

In April, 1935, the Bishop went on the air and proclaimed unequivocally that Father Coughlin was sound in doctrine and had his *imprimatur*. Now, a good many people suspect that the eloquent Father is a good deal stronger than his Bishop, who is now an old man and whose diocese received a terrific financial blow in the Detroit banking *débâcle*. Coughlin is the biggest money-raiser in the diocese. However, the theory that the Bishop is only a tool in the hands of a powerful underling overlooks the fact that Coughlin has no great influence in Michigan, not to mention some of the deeper currents of Church politics. Coughlin has an enormous following among Catholics in New England, especially in Massachusetts, where the Bourbonism of O'Connell apparently has alienated some of the bottom layers of Catholic laity. Outside of New England, Coughlin's greatest following is in the farming sections of the Middle West—and this is primarily a Protestant following.

Bishop Gallagher has a record of sturdy independence,

and many believe he is still smarting as a result of the restraints the Church applied to his zeal for Irish freedom during the war. However, one may be sure that he was not defying his superiors in the Church when he gave Coughlin's public utterances his unqualified endorsement. One may be sure, moreover, that Coughlin is a big enough problem to have been discussed at the Vatican. There is good reason for believing that not only conservative members of the hierarchy in this country but some prominent Catholic laymen, noted for their generous financial contributions, have tried to get Coughlin silenced via the Vatican. Possibly some of them found out that the Pope meant what he said in *Quadragesimo Anno,* and that the Vatican contains men much better versed in the world economic and political situation than the lay advisers of some of the Catholic bishops in the United States.

What the Church has not the slightest intention of permitting, is being drawn, as an issue, into American politics, through Father Coughlin, Al Smith, or anybody else. It was significant that simultaneously with Gallagher's public endorsement of Coughlin in April, 1935, Coughlin reiterated that the N.U.S.J. was not a political party. He conspicuously remained away from Milo Reno's Third Party round-up at Des Moines, at which the Kingfish was the chief speaker.

Coughlin has, so far, refused to commit himself or the N.U.S.J. to a Third Party program and has, instead, announced his desire to get results by bringing pressure to bear on Congress. Speaking at Detroit the same day that Huey Long offered to back Borah's choice (within limits) for the Presidency in 1936, Coughlin declared that "it is not our desire to form a political party, but it is our intention to drive out of public life the men who have promised us redress, who have preached to us the philosophy of social justice and, then, who have broken their promises to practice the philosophy of plutocracy."

While such a program of lobbying is calculated to assist Roosevelt, by relieving him of Congressional reactionaries, Coughlin disavowed the idea of one-party government under "the dictatorship of a President," explaining that the members of the National Union "reject atheistic Communism. We disavow racial Hitlerism; we turn our backs upon industrial Fascism. We have no part with plutocratic individualism and less with immoral capitalism as we find it in the United States today." This does not make his position much clearer but it does suggest that the hierarchy have definitely rejected the Third Party idea in favor of the traditional American institution of the lobby.

So long as Coughlin preaches from his text and observes discretion in his criticism of an admittedly faulty and unsatisfactory economic and social order, so long he will be permitted to turn the minds of multitudes of Americans—Jewish, Protestant and Catholic—in the direction of the social principles worked out by Leo XIII and Pius XI. But let him go that hair's breadth too far, which would convert his "lobby" of five million members of the National Union for Social Justice into a National Catholic Party, or let him presume to dictate a breach between the Catholics and the New Deal, and Father Coughlin will be silenced by his superiors. Two or three of the Father's closest friends have intimated that he will leave the Church, if necessary, to advance his social principles. Perhaps. Probably well over half his following is Protestant, anyway, and there is no doubt that he knows he is a powerful popular leader. Whether the Church or Coughlin would suffer more if he were unfrocked may be a debatable question, but unquestionably the clerical setting is one of Coughlin's most effective attributes. It would be

ironic indeed if the Church should try to rub out a priest
who has done more than any man in the United States to
publicize the social principles of Pope Pius XI. So long as
Gallagher remains Bishop of Detroit, the present arrange-
ment probably will be continued—whereby Coughlin has
a pretty free voice so long as he does not try to project himself as a candidate for office or as the leader of a political
party.

TARZAN OF THE EPIC

ALTHOUGH UPTON SINCLAIR, leader of the movement to "End Poverty in California"—the EPIC Plan which worried the California conservatives of 1934 to the point of desperation—was at one time a Marxian Socialist, his latest incarnation has a highly respectable and hundred per cent American lineage. It is the culmination of a point of view and a wave of agitation which began in the 1880's with Edward Bellamy's "Looking Backward" (one of F.D.R.'s political bibles), continued in the 1920's and early 1930's under the stimulus of Thorstein Veblen and the Technocrats, took a rather vague and mystical form in the Utopian movement, and blossomed in a concrete program for the abolition of poverty through production for use rather than for profit.

Edward Bellamy's epoch-making book was published in 1887, when the author was an active journalist in Springfield, Massachusetts (later he was an editorial writer on the "old" New York "Evening Post"). His works —"Looking Backward" and "Equality"—were widely translated and led to the formation of Bellamy Clubs, the first of which was established in Boston in 1888. By January, 1891, there were 162 such clubs organized to support the plan for nationalization of wealth and production for use that Bellamy outlined. His ideas persisted until they were given a scientific rationale by Veblen of America and Soddy of England and thus became the starting point of Technocracy.

As late as 1935, the Bellamy Clubs remained in existence, with headquarters at Springfield, Mass., and last
winter Bellamy's widow, a lady of seventy-three, came to
Washington to testify in behalf of the Lundeen unemployment insurance bill. Bellamy's daughter, Mrs. Marian
Farnshaw, is head of the Springfield Bellamy Club. These
Clubs made no claims to any particular strength and
their agitation, so far as Congress is concerned, has taken
the form of a few simple cards, mailed from various New
England points, outlining the "Bellamy Plan for all."

Equivalent to $5,000 for all, without money. How? Four
hours productive labor per day, five day week and 30 days
vacation with full income. Government ownership and operation of all industries (no unemployment, no poverty, no
crime), equal opportunity for all. Retire at 45 and still draw
your income. No politics, for all citizens; meet and talk it
over, then organize.

Although any detached analysis reveals a startling correspondence between some of the policies of the Roosevelt Administration—especially those of the F.E.R.A.—
and Bellamy's scheme for a Utopian economic democracy,
the movement, as such, has languished since Bellamy's
death in 1898 and is about as irrelevant to current politics
as is the Single-Tax Movement. Its vitality passed over
completely into the short-lived but momentous affair
known as Technocracy, which provided the real psychological curtain-raiser to the politics of plenty vs. the economics of scarcity, which formed the underlying drama of
the first two years of the New Deal.

II

In the summer of 1932 and winter of 1933 there occurred one of the strangest episodes in American history:

the advent, mushroom growth and suppression of Technocracy. Under the leadership of an extraordinary man named Howard Scott, a group of engineers and theorists —using Thorstein Veblen's findings as a basis and including such men as Steinmetz—had been working intermittently for ten years on the principle that modern technology had rendered both political and financial government obsolete and that, by permitting our machinery to function without adverse control of profiteers or politicians, we could achieve a far higher standard of living than ever before, with work and plenty for everyone.

It sounded like a dream but it happened to be true —in everything but human nature. Scott who had an unorthodox background of experience in Germany, Russia and Muscle Shoals, found converts, among them Leon Henderson, who is now Director of Research and Planning for the N.R.A. but was then employed by the Russell Sage Foundation, and Langdon W. Post, now Mayor LaGuardia's Commissioner of Tenement Housing but who had been defeated for the New York Assembly by Tammany and found time on his hands. Scott's engineering group was working on charts at Columbia University, while Scott himself was said to be elaborating an epoch-making Theory of Energy Determinants. The charts were later completed, most convincingly, by a group known as the Continental Committee, under Harold Loeb, as a relief project (sponsored by Post), but the Theory of Energy Determinants was never finally formulated by Scott. Instead, he fell a victim to his own love of publicity.

As his Technocratic theorem became known, the imagination of the whole country was fired. Technocratic leagues were formed and a lively literature sprang up overnight on the subject. It was to protect Scott and his work from this torrent of curiosity and interest that Post and others, including Fred Ackerman, Dal Hitchcock, John Carter, Quincy Howe and the son of Rabbi Wise, formed the Continental Committee on Technocracy. But Scott could not keep his mouth shut and he was as exhilarated by what went out of it as most men are by what entered it. He became publicity-drunk and delighted in making speeches. Finally, he said too much at the wrong time, his facts and figures were questioned, his overbearing truculence split up the group with which he was working, and there was a period of bickering and secession. The conservative press blandly announced that Technocracy was discredited and proved it by showing that poor Scott was bankrupt.

The majority of Americans believed the newspapers and laughed heartily over the quaint idea of an energy-currency based on ergs, which would give every man, woman and child an income based on current energy engaged in economic production equivalent to $10,000 a year in present values. Scott became more and more a laughing-stock and when the Continental Committee published its "Survey on Potential Product Capacity"—a study which completely dynamited the orthodox findings of the money-minded economists of the Brookings Institute on "America's Capacity to Produce"—it attracted little attention, although Charles A. Beard characterized the Loeb report as "the most important book of the twentieth century."

Yet Howard Scott and Technocracy started a current of thought which was swiftly to confront the Roosevelt Administration with its first, its greatest and its only real problem. Scott, tall, ungainly, tough in appearance, talking smoothly of ergs and energy determinants, might

have raided the Harper's Ferry of American capitalism
—the scientific arsenal on which modern wealth is based
—and been hung (in effigy) as a traitor to the profit-system,
but his soul went marching on. For a few dramatic weeks
he made the entire country realize that it was physically
possible for everyone to have plenty of everything. He
failed to last longer because he underestimated the American psychology which resolutely denies that two plus two
equals four and because he also overestimated his own
capacity for leadership, but he had fired the fuse which
led straight to the Utopian movement, to Upton Sinclair's EPIC Plan, to Dr. Townsend's Revolving Pensions
Plan and to acceptance of Huey Long's Share-Our-Wealth
program by wide masses of people.

This train of thought was destined to have a head-on
collision with Franklin Roosevelt in the opening days of
his Administration. Few people will ever realize how
close Roosevelt came to complete catastrophe on March
4, 1933. Technocracy had based its conclusions on the
assumption that the economic depression, under capitalism for private profit, was incurable, that the machines
would increase unemployment with growing acceleration, and that the profit system, as a result, was not so much
morally wrong as it was obsolete and irrelevant to our
economic methods.

Roosevelt, on the other hand, had been assured early
in the winter of 1933 that the worst of the depression was
over, that we were at the bottom of the dangerous
"curves" on the business charts, and that the "natural
forces of recovery" if supplemented by agricultural reforms would solve the crisis without the need for making
major changes. On this account, despite arguments that
he ought to lay plans for dealing with the approaching

collapse of the entire banking system and the paralysis of
our economic machinery, he approached the greatest
booby-trap in our history without plans and without
much more than the hope and purpose of making the
profit system work somehow, by extemporizing and patch-
ing up the worst of its defects. As a result, the group of
middle-class enthusiasts who had followed Scott soon
came to the conclusion that the New Deal was neither a
revolution nor a reform—but simply an interregnum between the collapse of the profit system and the construction of a Technocratic State, and proceeded to organize
for the coming scientific Utopia.

III

As Technocracy waned as a "discredited" political
force, its place was quickly taken by the Utopian movement, centering in Southern California like so many other
of the "joiner" groups.

The U.S.A. (Utopian Society of America, to you!) is,
in fact, a direct descendant of Technocracy. About Christ-
mas, 1932, during the depths of the interregnum, an organizer of retail sales for oil companies named Merritt J.
Kennedy, of Los Angeles, heard Manchester Boddy, the
editor of the Los Angeles "Daily Illustrated News," deliver a lecture on Technocracy. Boddy had been publishing a series of articles on the subject and had even gone
so far as to predict that the New Deal would apply Technocratic principles to the solution of the economic crisis.
It did not seem so unreasonable at the time. Scott was
still somewhat under control and the President-elect was
far from unsympathetic, although he shrewdly suspected
that after the nation's experience with "The Great Engi-

neer" anything which proposed government by technicians would be doubtful politics.

At any rate, Kennedy was moved by Boddy's lecture and hurried out to buy all the Technocratic literature he could find. He also interested his friend and neighbor, Eugene J. Reed, a former investment banker of Denver, itself a strong center of Technocratic sentiment. Together they attended Technocratic meetings and hoped until the late spring of 1933 that F.D.R. was going to put their principles into effect. As the N.R.A. took shape they sadly decided that they had been guilty of wishful thinking and began to consider ways of organizing a movement. Kennedy realized that Technocracy was still only a religious principle, which would have to be organized into a creed if it were to get anywhere. He also realized—and was frank to admit—that he and Reed, both of whom were without regular income at the time, needed to earn a living.

The nation which produces Elks and Masons, Red Men, Odd Fellows and Ku Kluxers knows how to organize in the territory north of the Rio Grande and west of the Alleghenies. Kennedy suggested that Reed write a ritual that would dramatize the evil power of the present money system based on debt and portray a new and higher order of life, with money based on production. In the meantime, Kennedy ran across another Technocrat, Walter H. Rousseau, a real estate promoter, who had written a little play called "Miss Technocracy," which had been produced by amateurs in Los Angeles. When Reed was taken ill, Rousseau finished writing the ritual for the new society, which was launched in the fall of 1933, on the heels of the plow-under campaign, the slaughter of the piglets, and the collapse of Hugh Johnson's ballyhooed "Blue Eagle" reëmployment drive.

The distinguishing feature of the U.S.A. is its secrecy
and its ritual—two formulas which have insured longevity
to many less worthy enterprises. The ritual is divided into
"cycles" and makes a profound impression on contemporary middle-class Americans, although its future appeal
may not be so great. The first two "cycles" are held in the
homes of members or in small halls. At the outset, the
candidates for membership raise their right hands and
pledge allegiance to the Constitution of the United States,
and swear to uphold the legal processes of the city, state
and nation, to observe the Golden Rule, to refrain from
hatred, malice and all uncharitableness against any man
in power, and to work for the overthrow of evil conditions, not of individuals. They are then asked certain
questions—rhetorical in character—which reflect sharp
criticism on the present economic system, such as, "Do
you believe necessities of life should be destroyed while
people are allowed to suffer want and privation?" "Do
you believe that poverty can be abolished without the
abolition of profit?" and "Do you think the N.R.A. members in your district are living up to their codes?"

Then the play begins. Into the darkened room come a
band of ragged persons representing dispossessed humanity, led by "Forgotten Man." They approach the house of
a grain merchant whose warehouses are overflowing and
offer their labor for food: the offer is rejected. They go
on, seeking clothes from a clothing merchant, and so on,
but are informed that they can get nothing without gold.
So they go to the money-lender, who says he will let them
have money on interest if they can give "security." Then
as they argue, men leap forward and put chains on their
legs, to get the money. The money-lender puts money
into their hands, but they soon discover that it is not gold,
but only paper and, as they move along, they are arrested

and fined for failing to pay taxes. That takes away their money. Then, as they proceed on the economic Via Crucis, they meet two men whom they recognize as the grain and clothing merchant who, in self-defense, shout that they also are penniless now. This ends the first and second cycles.

The third and fourth cycles, given on another night and usually in a larger hall, show the pilgrims, with their ex-capitalist friends, meeting a hermit named "Reason." After hearing their troubles, Reason guides them to the Land of Plenty for All. He explains that the "profit system" is as obsolete as monasteries and despotic kings, that times have changed and that, when everybody works to produce for use, everybody will have all he can use. They suddenly arrive in Utopia, which bears certain physical resemblances to Washington. The Department of the Interior is distributing needed commodities to all, instead of worrying about petty graft on P.W.A. projects; the Department of Industry is regulating the supply of needed goods on the principle of perpetual surplus; the Department of Commerce is abolishing competition; the Department of Labor is working to maintain production at the peak of efficiency; the Department of Education is assuring every child full development of his natural faculties (page Huey Long!); Foreign Trade is bartering surplus goods with foreign countries; National Defense is striving to promote international peace.

In this Technocratic Utopia, the people own all the means of production. Each citizen gets a certificate of production entitling him to an equal share of all the necessities and luxuries of life that are produced and this certificate must be spent within a year (page Doc Townsend!). Up to the age of twenty-five, every boy and girl is educated and given physical training. For the next twenty

years, everyone follows self-chosen occupations. After the
age of forty-five, anyone who wants to retire can do so, but
there is no obligation. Crime has disappeared; there are
no debts and no individual savings. It is all very nice. Reason rips the chains off the pilgrims and says to the Forgotten Man, "Now you are the Man Who Found Himself!"

At this point, the initiates are full-fledged members of
the Society, liable to pay a fee of $3 plus dues of ten cents
a month (though few of them do so). There is a fifth
cycle, which is still secret (as the first four cycles originally were), but only those who keep up their dues and
bring in enough new members are allowed to see it.

By this system, the U.S.A. proposes to "educate the
American people along economic lines so that, by the use
of reason and the ballot, rather than by the use of hate
and bomb, it may bring about a readjustment in national
economic thinking, placing human values before bond
values, by stressing production for use rather than for
profit." The movement urges a letter-campaign directed
to President Roosevelt, praising the New Deal but urging
a production-for-use system, based on nationalization of
the productive plant, assignment of labor and substitution of "effort money" for the metallic-backed currency
and bank-credit of the present system.

Despite the vagueness and educational character of its
approach, the U.S.A. is no inconsiderable force. Its first
meeting was held early in the summer of 1934, when 25,-
000 jammed the Hollywood Bowl and many more were
turned away. The movement spread like wildfire amid the
ruined or badly battered lower middle class of Southern
California. Its reliance on secrecy, symbolism and religion
marks it as a genuine expression of their aspirations. At
first it was helped by the myth that it had been started by

Roosevelt himself, or by his Brain Trust. Then it was charged that Upton Sinclair had started it, and it is a fact that Sinclair sought and received U.S.A. support. Late in 1934, it spread more rapidly, getting as many as 5,000 new members a day, until in last November, when national headquarters opened in New York, it had 600,000 members, acquired by an ingenious "snowball system" in which each member has to bring in two more persons to each meeting. Since then, however, its drive has slackened, partly as a result of Sinclair's defeat and partly because of its lack of dynamic leadership. Another factor may be its lack of definition. It can't be packed into a single bill and its real importance seems to lie in its educational quality and its ability to indoctrinate the principle of production for use as a semi-religious injunction.

Aside from this, its chief significance in current politics is the fact that it demonstrated the vitality of the purpose to abolish the "profit system" among wide sections of the American public. It picked up where the Technocrats originally failed and, under disinterested and sincere if rather sapless leadership, took the Technocratic religion and made it a semi-political force sufficiently powerful to be an important element in the dramatic campaign of Upton Sinclair for the Governorship of California.

IV

The Sinclair campaign was the most sensational political development of 1934.

This ex-Socialist reformer, muckraker, pamphleteer, author, motion-picture producer and dreamer accepted at face value the more liberal interpretations of the New Deal. Previously he had run, on the Socialist ticket, for Congressman, Governor and Senator, but had never scraped together more than 60,000 of California's 2,200,000-odd votes. Then, in the summer of 1933, he decided to become a New Deal Democrat. Sinclair, it should be noted, is fundamentally a preacher, a reformer on the order of the Old Testament prophets, a Protestant and lay Father Coughlin.

His campaign began with the publication of "I, Governor of California" and the outline of his EPIC Plan. It was received with deafening silence. He kept on, speaking and writing and organizing EPIC Clubs, until the late spring of 1934, when he announced himself as candidate for the Democratic nomination. The official New Deal Democrats—the McAdoo outfit—nominated George Creel, Wilson's war-time chief of propaganda, a liberal who had been one of the little band of aides to McAdoo at Chicago in 1932. The old-line native son Democrats (McAdoo's strength was in Southern California) put up Justus Wardell, who had unsuccessfully but gallantly led the effort to deliver the California delegation to Roosevelt at Chicago in 1932. Sinclair was a rank outsider who didn't have a chance.

By the middle of the summer, however, the rest of the country suddenly realized that a political miracle was being "passed" in California. General Hugh Johnson had endorsed Creel, and Jim Farley and his gang had done everything they could do, discreetly, to let it be known that Creel was the Administration candidate. Then, on August 28, 1934, Sinclair carried the Democratic primary with a whoop. He beat all his opponents—there were several minor candidates in addition to Creel and Wardell—decisively and with a clear majority over their combined votes, getting 438,000 ballots, the largest number ever received by any Democrat in a California primary.

The ex-Socialist, the man who had awakened the country to the meat scandals thirty years ago with "The Jungle," had captured the Democratic Party in the State which assured the election of Woodrow Wilson in 1916.

This aroused the nation, made no end of trouble for Big Jim and F.D.R., and touched off one of the most ominous and explosive campaigns in American political history. It was explosive because Sinclair, in his EPIC Plan, had reduced the fact of American plenty to a concrete political program and demonstrated its ability to wreck established systems and traditions. It was ominous because it demonstrated how the American press—even the so-called "liberal" press—will prostitute its news-columns and join in a bitter Fascist lynching-bee under a little provocation.

The campaign was bitter and vindictive in the extreme. The conservatives represented Sinclair as the dynamiter of churches and forged "Communist" manifestoes urging the "Comrades" to vote for Sinclair. In an article written after his defeat, Sinclair remarked that, according to the "lie factory":

I am a Communist, an advocate of free love, an enemy of religion, a jackass, a nut, a self-advertiser out for personal gain. . . . About the kindest and gentlest thing they could say of me was that I am a dangerous and impractical visionary who would lead the state to destruction.

In return, Sinclair's "EPIC News" struck back at these lies as "obviously the products of nitwits, psychopathics with a persecution complex, disgruntled racketeers, low-grade crooks, third-rate Hessians, deflated megalomaniacs." This exchange of compliments reminded the country that Upton Sinclair, now aged fifty-six, is still the nation's most expert muckraking pamphleteer, and that he shows no sign of let-up in his long crusade for social justice.

In thirty-five years he has turned out forty-nine books, as well as innumerable pamphlets and articles, all flaming with moral indignation, and nearly all containing a good deal of inaccuracy and exaggeration. He became a national figure as long ago as 1906, with the publication of "The Jungle," when he was invited to the White House by Theodore Roosevelt. Since then he has functioned as a sort of socialistic Tarzan, swinging rapidly out of the reach of the great reptiles and carnivores which haunt our jungle economy, rebuking the manifest iniquities of American life and seeking perfection by nearly every kind of cult known to the fertile brain of man.

He entered the California primary as an exponent of New Deal theories, and his EPIC Plan contained no elements which were markedly out of tune with the Rooseveltian policies. He proposed, in brief, to put the unemployed to work in vacant factories and on unused land, in order to produce their own goods and to raise their own food. He argued that this system was the most logical and most economical and could be reconciled with capitalism by paying rent to the owners of the land and factories, at a gigantic saving over current relief costs. (He apparently underestimated the vested interest that the capitalists claimed in a right to be paid for feeding and clothing the unemployed, out of relief funds, and their right to rely on the potential labor of the workers as a basis for existing wage scales.) Under EPIC, the land-colonies would be established and directed by the California Authority for Land (CAL). The factories would be operated under the California Authority for Production (CAP). A public body called the California

Authority for Money (CAM) would finance CAP and CAL.

The costs of this and of a system of old age pensions of $50 a month, and of relief for the blind and the physically disabled, were to be borne by a State income tax, steeply graduated on incomes from $5,000 a year up, and by an inheritance tax taking 50 per cent of every individual bequest over $50,000 and 50 per cent of every estate over $250,000. While taxes on privately-owned utilities and on unimproved land (here there is an echo of the Single Tax) were to be hiked, all homes and ranches assessed at $3,000 or less would be tax exempt. Until this tax system could start functioning, Sinclair proposed to finance EPIC by issuing scrip, on the basis of economic production in his socialistic colonies, which scrip could be accepted by railroads, etc., and turned in to the State Government for taxes.

He also proposed to make a clean sweep of vigilante prejudices by pardoning Tom Mooney, still serving a life sentence in San Quentin prison for the Preparedness Parade Bomb in 1916, despite ample proof of his conviction on perjured testimony.

The Sinclair candidacy put Roosevelt on a hot spot. After consultation with the beaten Creel and other Democratic experts, it was decided that Sinclair should be supported if he would modify his program and accept a platform which could be approved by the National Administration. Sinclair lived up to his share of the bargain. He produced "Immediate EPIC" and secured its approval by the post-primary Democratic State Convention. The modified plan dropped the temporary scrip feature—which was probably unconstitutional, anyhow—and toned down the harsh outline of EPIC's production-for-use program to softer contours more acceptable to the producers for profit. The main features were, however, left in the plan, including the device of putting the unemployed to work in leased factories and on leased or purchased land.

In all this, Sinclair could quite properly maintain that he was in full accord with the New Deal, since Harry Hopkins' F.E.R.A. was doing exactly the same thing that EPIC proposed to do, in a number of places. It was doing it openly in Ohio and was planning to undertake it on a large scale in the vicinity of Washington. It was putting the unemployed to work on a huge scale, in canning meats, making mattresses and clothes, and so on, and it was supervising a rural rehabilitation and subsistence homestead system by which dispossessed farmers and farm laborers got back on the land from which the profit system had driven them.

Sinclair also emphasized the fact that his plan was much cheaper than the continuation of the dole or work relief. This argument was widely ridiculed, but he was obviously right that it would cost less money to have the unemployed clothe and feed each other by their own labor than to buy food and clothing for them with relief funds. After the November elections, Harry Hopkins barnstormed the country telling business men who wanted to economize on relief costs that a cheaper form of relief was to set the unemployed to work making their own things. Curiously enough, business men decided that they didn't want cheap relief at any price which would involve a reduction in F.E.R.A.'s purchases from private business —again the vested *commercial* interest in the dole which is an ominous feature of that system.

At any rate, Sinclair adopted the modified EPIC Plan and stood by his bargain. Later in the campaign, when it seemed expedient to abandon him, the Roosevelt people made much of the assertion that he had "run out" and gone back to advocating original EPIC in violation of his agreement. This excuse was pretty lame. Sinclair did indicate that the modified EPIC was only intermediate to the original EPIC, but that was no more than was required by practical politics, in view of the enthusiasm of his followers for the original plan, and was also a perfectly normal adaptation of the principle of "gradualism" to social reforms.

As a matter of fact, the Roosevelt-Sinclair love-feast was only grin-deep. After his nomination, Sinclair came East to meet the President, and the latter wanted to be on friendly terms with a man who had brought such voting strength into the Democratic Party and had won control of that party in so important a State as California. The two men had a long, friendly talk at Hyde Park, from which Sinclair emerged spouting praise of the wonders of F.D.R. Then he ran down to New York, where he had a lovely talk with Jim Farley, and on to Washington, where he saw Hopkins, Ickes and other big shots of the New Deal left wing. He got plenty of encouragement but no promises of campaign support. Hopkins, in his usual impulsive manner, blurted out to the press his own hope that Sinclair would be elected. "He's on our side, isn't he?" asked Hopkins. The question answered itself.

Sinclair was on the side of the New Deal. He went to extremes in order to control his rather undisciplined nature and become a loyal lieutenant in a national liberal movement under Roosevelt. It was true that he needed Roosevelt's help to be elected Governor of California in 1934 but it is also true that Roosevelt may need Sinclair's help to carry California in 1936—and California decided the fateful election of 1916. It is a fact that Roosevelt deserted Sinclair, for reasons which seemed convincing at the time—an act which may prove to be a greater blunder than Hughes' historic snubbing of Hiram Johnson in 1916. Naturally, Roosevelt counts on Hiram to deliver

California to him in 1936. Hiram, having gathered every nomination, except the Socialist and Communist, for the Senatorship in 1934, kept his hands off the fight for the Governorship, although a word from him would have elected Sinclair. Hiram is a potent figure and a great progressive "boss" but in an open test of popular following between him and the EPIC Tarzan it is by no means certain that Johnson would have a walk-over.

The apparent reasons which led Roosevelt to desert Sinclair are persuasively advanced by apologists for the Administration in this episode.

There is no percentage in backing a loser, especially if that loser is too closely identified with your policies.

It is, moreover, bad politics for a President to tangle up in State fights. It is true that Roosevelt gave a left-handed endorsement to Bob LaFollette and that he tried to keep on friendly terms with Olson and Shipstead, the Farmer-Labor leaders, although in the latter case his political mechanics, Farley and Hurja, backed the regular Democratic candidates. It is also true that, through Farley, he tried to defeat Bronson Cutting in New Mexico, and failed. But, the general strike in San Francisco had made California pretty jumpy, and both precedent and common sense dictated that the President should not get out too far on the EPIC limb in California where there was a fair possibility of a Fascist *coup d'état* if Sinclair should be elected.

Moreover, Sinclair's modified EPIC, though perfectly consistent with the New Deal, was not identical with the program on which Roosevelt was working, and although it was true that the latter had set the unemployed to work in producing their own goods, he had never regarded these "islands of socialism" as more than safety-zones, and proposed instead to enable everybody to get a job in the capitalistic system. His real approach to the problem is to set the unemployed to work at conserving natural resources, improving the national plant, developing those long-range projects which are necessary for future prosperity but which, because they operate over several generations, offer no appeal to the profit motive, and to let the unemployed buy their goods through the regular channels. His $4,880,000,000 work relief program is the New Deal alternative to EPIC.

Accordingly, Roosevelt was merely pleasant to Sinclair and if Sinclair believed that Roosevelt promised to issue a statement or make a speech on "production for use" before the end of the campaign—which would have helped Sinclair's candidacy immensely—it was probably just another of those misunderstandings that grow out of Roosevelt's affability. Certainly, the statement was not made. Farley, on the other hand, maintained officially the correct machine politician's point of view. He told the politicians who inquired as to his attitude: "Sinclair won in the primary. The party should support the popular choice."

However, before the post-primary campaign had far advanced, Roosevelt was badly on the spot. While Sinclair had dodged the general strike issue by saying that if he had been Governor there would have been no occasion for the strike, the conservative leaders of California —the Gianninis, Hearst, Harry Chandler—began sounding the tocsin of Red Revolution in the Grizzly Bear Republic of the Golden West. Supported by the vigilantes, the Native Sons and the traditional Republican crowd— including the Recluse of Palo Alto—the press was a unit against Sinclair. Not only the Hearst and the other traditional Red-baiting newspapers of California raised the hue-and-cry but the so-called "liberal" journals joined in the *battue*. Roy Howard, head of Scripps-Howard, took a special carload of "trained seals" from the East to "beat Sinclair," leaving behind Heywood Broun, who was openly for Sinclair.

Sinclair did not have a single newspaper in his favor and most of them were so virulently opposed to his candidacy that they perverted their news columns. Not since the World War had the press so scandalously and ominously prostituted itself on behalf of the status quo. At the same time, Roosevelt was subjected to constant pressure to repudiate Sinclair. The Giannini interests, among the chief backers of the New Deal on the West Coast, went to lengths to secure a White House rebuff to the official Democratic candidate in California. Roosevelt held off until he saw that Sinclair would probably be licked, if only on the old American principle which holds, "I do not care who casts my country's votes, so long as I may count them." Then Sinclair was repudiated, via a statement from George Creel, and Jim Farley followed suit by repudiating the "blonde stenographer's error" which had resulted in a letter urging support of the full ticket, including Sinclair. This letter had reached California and been published in Sinclair's "EPIC News." At the same time that the forces supporting the Republican candidate, Frank Merriam, were attacking Sinclair as a Communist and an atheist, the Communists, and even the orthodox New York Socialists of the Norman Thomas school, derided him. Altogether it was a disgraceful performance and a sardonic travesty on the meaning of democracy when a candidate proposes an orderly change in economic arrangements.

Even so, the issue was in doubt up to the end and Merriam, to help in the fight, had to come out with a ringing endorsement of the Townsend Plan for Old Age Revolving Pensions of $200 a month, thus cutting into Sinclair's

Southern California vote. Raymond L. Haight, the Progressive-Commonwealth nominee, tried to hold a middle ground between the Republican reactionaries and the radicals and met the usual fate of middle-grounders. He failed to win Sinclair's radical following, while many conservatives who preferred him to Merriam voted for the latter for safety's sake. In spite of all this, Sinclair more than doubled his primary vote, making large gains in Central California, where labor was bitter against Merriam and his reactionary backers as a result of the suppression of the General Strike.

The official count was:

Merriam (*Republican*)	1,138,000
Sinclair (*Democratic*)	879,000
Haight (*Commonwealth*)	302,000

Merriam is a minority governor.

EPIC did not die with the election. The logic and popular pressure behind it are so strong that Merriam indicated that he would adopt part of the plan as a matter of temporary necessity. Contrary to his campaign pledges, he was forced to come in with a higher tax program, for which he was sternly rebuked by the Republican newspapers, even though the emphasis was on the sales tax and not on incomes. Yet the forces of the EPIC campaign are still strong and are organized in every county and most precincts, under a program to recall State Legislators and officials and to employ the initiative and referendum on a wide scale to enforce the Plan. July, 1935, has been tentatively set as the deadline, a fact which probably accounts for the feverish reports of optimism and prosperity which drift back East from the Pacific Coast, as possible advance-signs of a psychological movement to identify the G.O.P. with good times, as of yore.

Sinclair is not through. After publishing a new book,

"I, Candidate for Governor, and How I Got Licked," he prepared to move again at the right time, which may be this summer and again may be in 1936. While indicating that he might not again be a political candidate, he did not lay aside his new-found career as a political boss. There is little doubt that he cannot easily be dislodged from his majority control of the Democratic Party in California, if he keeps his wits about him. He is not talking of a Third-Party movement except as a possibility if Roosevelt continues to dicker with the bankers and political stand-patters and continues a policy of scarcity. Sinclair is on the inside of the Democratic Party for the present, whether the machine Democrats welcome him or not. If he sees a chance to close with poor old Frank Merriam, he might use the California initiative and referendum to nip in and repeal the sales tax and replace it with a tax on wealth.

It is hard to imagine Sinclair—with his intense sincerity, his crystalline intellect and his personal asceticism—supporting Huey Long in 1936. He is too much of a Socialist to have anything to do with anything which even remotely suggests Fascism. But both he and Long might find a satisfactory third candidate, and if so, Sinclair's indefatigable typewriter, his fluent and crackling phraseology, and his reputation for disinterested public spirit, would be a force to be reckoned with in a national campaign. He would prefer, however, to go along with Roosevelt, but only on the condition that the latter salvages the New Deal and moves it far enough to the left in 1936 to arouse the enthusiasm of Southern California. That this may be necessary in any case, and irrespective of EPIC, is suggested by that other "Plan" produced in Southern California—Dr. Townsend's Old Age Revolving Pensions.

THE TOWNSEND SAGA

THE TOWNSEND PLAN—that scheme for Old Age Revolving Pensions which swept out of the West in 1934 like a dust-storm in the wake of a generation of the blistering economics of untrammeled greed—began in a garbage can, but the scrawny, humble man of sixty-eight who originated the plan and now, somewhat to his bewilderment, finds himself becoming a Messiah to millions of people, is symbolic, in his antecedents and his own history, of the epic of the nation.

Dr. Francis E. Townsend was born in a log cabin in Fairbury, Illinois, of early American stock. (His great-great-grandfather Townsend won a place in history by putting a chain across the Hudson River to keep the British fleet out of New York during the Revolutionary War.) After an elementary education in local schools he began to roam, trying everything from teaching school to homesteading. At the age of 26 he showed up at the Omaha Medical School with a few dollars in his pocket and the determination to become a doctor. For four years he worked his way through medical school, doing everything from cutting grass and tending furnaces to delivering newspapers. With the true instinct of the frontiersman he went shortly after his graduation to the cowboy and mining Black Hills section of South Dakota. He had a horse-and-buggy practice, supplemented by a small hospital that he operated in partnership with another physician. He married a nurse in the hospital, a widow with

seven children. They had three children of their own and
adopted another. After many years of hard work they
moved, some years ago, to Long Beach, California, where
Townsend got a job in the city health department. The
salary was modest and the work kept him indoors. Taking
advantage of one of the periodic Southern California
epidemics of real estate fever, he offered his services to
a young real estate and loan broker, R. E. Clements, who
was thirty years his junior. Townsend moved serenely
through the high pressure of competition in real estate
salesmanship. He was seldom able to close a deal without business-like assistance, but people seemed to like
him and he did reasonably well until the depression, followed by the Los Angeles earthquake, cast a blight on
realtors.

This left Townsend with plenty of time on his hands at
a time when Southern California was boiling with new
movements and new ideas for economic reform. And it
left him plenty of time to speculate on the history of the
nation and the successive movements which had carried
his family across the continent in the course of 150 years.
Being a thoughtful man who had worked his own way up
from a log cabin and had performed his duties to a large
family with modest success, he was distressed by what he
saw and heard about the plight of the country. Then, one
day, he saw three old women rummaging through a garbage can. This in the salubrious climate of Southern
California was the ultimate degradation of the American
dream—the dream that had brought his ancestors to the
New World and sustained their descendants as they made
their way across the continent. Doc Townsend let out a
cry that brought his wife running to his side. He swore
with a vehemence which dumbfounded her. And being
of self-reliant old pioneering stock, he sat down right

away to try to find some way to wipe out this disgrace to the American heritage. He did it with all the self-confidence of a country doctor preparing to remove an appendix on the kitchen table of a South Dakota shanty.

Townsend soon calculated that if all the old people were given enough for a decent, if modest, mode of life, the demand for goods would be sufficient to end the depression. This was the origin of the Townsend Plan. It sprang, not from the shrewdness of a demagogue, or publicity seeker, but from a deep sense of social injustice in the heart of a self-reliant member of the American lower middle class.

Somewhere or other the good doctor picked up the statement that in 1929 the people of the United States did a gross business of $935,000,000,000, and by a little figuring he saw that a turnover tax of 2 per cent on this sum would produce almost twenty billion dollars or about enough to give $200 a month to every person over the age of 60. He read enough of the spending theory of recovery —on which both Hoover and Roosevelt worked in the initial years of the depression—to see that his scheme could be worked into a glitteringly sanitary plan for making the capitalist system come back to life and work, without any material reform in the matter of private ownership, private profit or concentration of control.

Doc Townsend had located the shortest of short-cuts. Under his Old Age Revolving Pensions there would be no need for socialization, control of production, social credit or any other doctrine or device. He claimed that by enabling the aged to live in comfort his plan would give every young man a job and thus restore prosperity, with only a moderate boost in the cost of living—24 per cent— as a sort of premium to provide national old age insurance. It would be cheap at twice the price, he felt.

He took his scheme down to his boss, Mr. Clements. At first Clements was skeptical—first converts are notoriously difficult—but, as Townsend explained it, Clements began to think that there might be something to the idea —perhaps especially as it appeared that it might make it possible to reduce real estate taxes. Clements, who, with Townsend, shares the honor of the Townsend Plan, is described as a "mental prodigy" by his friends. He is, as a matter of record, a native of Amarillo, Texas, and a product of the Fort Worth High School. At any rate, he bent his great brain to three or four weeks of studying statistics and economics in the public library and eventually reappeared with the statement that the idea was sound. He then sat him down with Doc Townsend and together they wrote out the Townsend Old Age Revolving Pension Plan. This was in the closing days of the first year of the New Deal, after the major Roosevelt experiments had been launched and the pledge of a more abundant life had been written into national policy.

On New Year's Day, 1934, Townsend and Clements went together to a vacant room in the office building of a friend, Townsend carrying a pail of blue paint, Clements a pail of gray paint. Together they painted the floor and base-board, let the paint dry, moved in a desk, a stenographer and typewriter, and set to work mailing out letters describing the plan. No one who has never staked his future on the response of the American people to a new political idea can appreciate the utter pathos of their position. Would it be another flash in the pan? Answers began to dribble back at the rate of two or three letters a day. The men kept at it and in a few weeks answers were coming in at the rate of a hundred a day.

From this they mounted rapidly until now, about 2,000 letters a day are received at O.A.R.P. National Headquarters in Los Angeles and an office force of one hundred people is required to handle correspondence and the staff work involved in one of the greatest popular responses recorded in national politics.

As the letters accumulated, they got the idea of the Townsend Clubs, more perhaps as a way of eliminating strain on headquarters than with any specific political purpose. They were to be neighborhood clubs and consisted of two different kinds: "Minor" clubs with less than 100 members, "Major" clubs with up to 1,000 members. After a thousand members, a new club is supposed to be started.

Unlike Huey Long's "Share-Our-Wealth" groups—and incidentally the Townsendites are ultra-respectable in their attitude toward the Kingfish—the Townsend Clubs are supported by dues, the organizer of each group collecting 25 cents from each member as a year's dues payable in advance. When he gets 100 members, he sends in their names, keeps $7.50 for himself, and remits the remaining $17.50 to national headquarters for the pamphlets, bulletins and so forth which are sent to the club members. The Townsend crowd claim that this $17.50 isn't quite enough to cover the cost of the service until after a club rises above 100 members, when they begin to accumulate a margin for general organization and publicity expenses, since they are saved the cost of a second club permit and various other initial charges. At any rate, according to the financial statement, certified by public accountant, of the National Headquarters, which are incorporated as Old Age Revolving Pensions, they received a total of approximately $85,000 during the last eleven months of 1934, indicating a paid-up membership of about 500,000 recruited during this period.

There seems to be no particular racket involved. Both

Townsend and Clements say they draw $50 a month each as salary, plus travel-expenses when they are barn-storming for O.A.R.P. They claim a total of about 3,500 clubs, being especially strong in California, Oregon, Washington, the Rocky Mountain States, Minnesota (which contains 500 clubs), and are spreading rapidly in Ohio, Indiana, Michigan and New England. They don't maintain complete membership files, on the ground that it is a needless expense.

The movement differs from the Huey Long and the Upton Sinclair get-togethers in that neither Townsend nor Clements is a candidate for the Presidency or for any other major public office. Instead, they are following the well-charted lines of nonpartisan pressure-group politics, as worked out by the Anti-Saloon League, the World War Veterans and the American Federation of Labor. The Townsendites support the candidates of either party who favor their plan and oppose those who don't.

Townsend repeatedly has been urged by his supporters to announce himself as a Presidential candidate. But he consistently has subordinated himself, and his weekly publication reiterates in every issue that he will not be a candidate and that the Townsend movement must be kept free of personal political ambitions. In March, 1935, when some of his enthusiastic aides declared that they intended to run him for the Presidency, he promptly issued a flat refusal even to consider the possibility, adding: "I have neither the mental nor the physical equipment to be President."

In January, 1935, Townsend, Clements and the latter's pretty red-headed wife (who also works in the O.A.R.P. organization) felt strong enough to move on Washington. The New Deal's draft of social security legislation had made old age pensions on the European model practical politics. They opened headquarters in a small office in the Southern Building and printed the lettering on the door of their office in small black capitals, because Mrs. Clements felt that large gold letters were too expensive. Fame of their movement had preceded them to the national capital, by several months, and they found the politicians in an anxious mood.

The Townsend movement had been so powerful in California last autumn that Frank Merriam felt compelled to endorse it in his fight with Sinclair, who had a much more modest scale of pensions in mind. Merriam's endorsement may, in fact, have been chiefly responsible for his election. In February—by an easy piece of buck-passing—the California State Legislature memorialized the Federal Government to adopt the plan. Wise politicians said that if Merriam had failed to recommend this course he would have been recalled.

It would be a mistake to assume that the Townsend movement is confined to the Townsend Clubs. In addition to its permanent paid membership, it circulates petitions which anybody may sign and claims to have secured between twenty and thirty-five million signatures on these petitions. Allowing for Southern Californian enthusiasm, it is safe to assume that they have several million signatures. In addition to the petitions, they have organized a letter-writing campaign to State Legislators and Congressmen. In the early months of 1935, they laid down on Congressmen, especially on the Westerners, the greatest barrage of personal letters in Congressional history. It caused some hairs to turn white and other hairs to be torn out by their despairing roots.

This was followed by the introduction of a 1,500-word bill by Representative McGroarty of California, incorporating the O.A.R.P. Plan. Townsend himself came on to

Washington on the crest of a wave of agitation. He had never had to make a speech in his life, but in 1934 he went out and explained his plan to his clubs. At first he needed the coaching on voice, gestures and delivery that Mrs. Townsend, Mrs. Clements and other friends supplied, but he quickly reached the depressingly inevitable point where a man likes to hear himself speak, and built up a personal confidence which has helped him address crowds of as many as ten thousand people. His stock address—all good agitators from Demosthenes down have been men of one speech—is a quaint blend of Biblical Christianity and hazy economics, culminating in an exhortation to "Honor thy father and thy mother" and to preserve "enlightened democracy" rather than sink into "the chaos of a Fascist dictatorship or a bloody dictatorship of the proletariat."

The strain of this campaign had so worn down his slender body that when the House Ways and Means Committee wanted to question him closely on his Plan, he was able to plead ill-health.

The conservatives in Congress, and throughout the East in general, tried the familiar Three "R's" of reaction: Ridicule, Refutation and Rough Stuff. Denunciation and ridicule got precisely nowhere, for the very sound political reason that in a democracy nothing that has so many votes behind it in the home districts is ridiculous. Then a few more intelligent journalists decided that the Townsend movement was serious and required a serious answer. While Mark Sullivan turned in the old line fire alarm, Walter Lippmann tried to show up its fallacies but got tangled up in one or two fundamental economic fallacies himself. A few others tried the same labor of love, with greater statistical success, but discovered that O.A.R.P.—like the Bonus—is not the sort of movement which can be demolished on conventional fiscal grounds. This is because, despite its emotionalism and despite the vital flaws which can be discovered in its mechanism, it is based on the essential fact that there is enough in this country to provide a comfortable living for everyone. No economic or political institution is sufficiently strong to stand up against the tremendous fact of American abundance and the only way to counteract the "unsound" features of movements like the O.A.R.P. is to espouse some more workable scheme to provide everybody with a comfortable living—and damned quick, too!

For old people approaching or over sixty aren't the only ones behind the plan. Hundreds of thousands—millions—of young people have been drawn behind it because they think it will clear the way for them to get the good jobs vacated by the old people and will produce general prosperity within a year, without "regimentation." A few of them may hope to live on the old folks' pensions but, judging by each generation's impatience with parental control when that control is expressed financially, it is not likely that this is a major consideration.

Hence the Townsend Plan is sweeping the country and it offers to the New Dealers a suggestion as to the necessary character of any program which is designed to arouse public support and enthusiasm. It is concrete—for the general Rooseveltian "more abundant life" it substitutes "$200 a month"—and so simple to put into operation, according to its sponsors, that it would dynamite the depression within a year. It can be embraced in a single Act of Congress, for the passage of which its supporters can lobby, whereas the Utopians, for example, haven't got the foggiest idea of how to get from "here" to "there"—the base problem of progressive politics. It is not socialistic but preserves private ownership and so appeals to the essentially conservative lower middle class. It is bold. It has a strong sentimental and semi-religious appeal and is so phrased as to appeal to all classes and age-groups.

On this account, it constitutes the most telling criticism of the Roosevelt Administration's old age pension plan—$30 a month for people over seventy—and, by raising the ante, lifts itself from the category of stop-gap State socialism into that of a "complete" plan for ending the depression. It is the first such "complete plan" that has been presented to hundreds of thousands of reasonably intelligent people, in a form which they could understand and which did not violate many of their prejudices. More important still—from the solid political point of view—there is no conventional demagoguery in the movement. Townsend is not an orator, doesn't pretend to be a Savior, doesn't attempt the literary and psychological gymnastics of a Huey Long or an Upton Sinclair. The leaders of O.A.R.P. subordinate themselves to their movement, which thus takes the form of a powerful idea, sincerely offered, and with stupendous mass-backing.

And—again—it is not a racket. For over a year, Townsend's aides have been urging him to hike the membership dues in his clubs but so far he has refused on the ground that he wants no more than is needed to conduct the campaign for Old Age Revolving Pensions. For special expenses, special contributions are solicited, but the local clubs finance their own petitions and letter-writing campaigns. They have had some trouble with petty grafters and probably haven't collected all the money which should have been forwarded to headquarters. There was trouble in the New England branches, where some organizers decided to incorporate as a separate organization, but most of the Townsend Clubs remained loyal to the Doc.

He helps keep in touch with his followers through the "Townsend Weekly," started in January, 1935, with 125,-000 paid subscribers ($2.00 a year) accumulated in six weeks. To witness the pristine respectability of the movement, Kathleen Norris, the writer who has a literary strangle-hold on motherhood for the better-paid women's magazines, contributed a fifteen-hundred-word article to the January 21 issue of the "Townsend Weekly." She made a stirring plea for the plan, reporting that study had supplanted her previous skepticism with glowing faith and that "The Townsend Plan—audacious, original, inspired, has no blow-holes."

The Townsend movement has effectively expressed itself as a political force. Last March, after the House Committee had manhandled and "dismissed" the idea, a shudder ran through Washington, D. C., when inconspicuous despatches to the eastern papers reported that a member of the Oregon State Legislature had been recalled for failing to support the Townsend Plan—the first time the recall had been used on a member of the Legislature. This is more than the Veterans, the Anti-Saloon League or the A.F. of L. had been able to do to people who had opposed them.

As a matter of fact, when Townsend struck Washington he found that he had a lot of "friends." A considerable number of shrewd and wealthy men have been trying to string along with Townsend on the side, because they want to get his sales tax adopted and thus avoid larger income and inheritance taxes. As soon as Townsend discovered their game he modified his plan so as to retain, and even to increase, income and inheritance taxes in the higher brackets. Then a number of Congressmen began to "educate" him in a sympathetic way. They didn't want to vote for his plan but feared that the Townsendites would knife them if they didn't. Instead, they tried to tone it down—reduce the pensions to $100 or $75 a month —a proposal which would eliminate its recovery features and turn it into a simple hand-out to the old folks. Despite hardy denials to his followers, Townsend did submit—or was forced to submit—to a modification of his plan in order to get Congressional support. The modified bill, submitted as an amendment to the Roosevelt social security bill, took a bad beating on its test in the House. General business recovery and the Administration's old age pensions may whittle down the Townsend strength in the next year, but it is unlikely that the movement will fade out of sight before the elections of 1936.

As matters stand, the Townsend crowd propose to support whichever Presidential candidate will endorse their plan. A sound progressive—even Roosevelt—would be their preference, as they privately admit that they would prefer to support a more "respectable" man than Huey Long. At any rate, they muster several million votes for the gathering of any politician who is clever enough to devise a policy which will satisfy their aspirations or who is desperate enough to promise what he knows he can't deliver. Doc Townsend has started something, for his plan represents a movement which will not stop until the American people get their heart's desire or until they are so apathetic as to accept penury in a land of plenty.

V

VIKING INVADER

FLOYD BJERNSTJERNE OLSON, Farmer-Labor Governor of Minnesota, is leader in his own right of a "Third Party" which like the LaFollette Progressive Party in near-by Wisconsin has become the "First Party" of the State. Hence he is under no obligations to the bugbear of conformity which inhibits political secession in the two-Party areas and must be considered—conciliated or beaten—on his own terms.

Those terms are formidable, for Olson describes himself as being "radical as hell" and his Party's program frankly proposes to substitute coöperative socialism of the Scandinavian type for the rather devastated regions of the simon-pure profit system in the northern Mississippi Valley region—which is admittedly the decisive political region of the country.

Olson is a Viking of forty-four. His father was born in Norway, his mother in Sweden, his wife is Czech, his daughter bears the Irish name of Patricia and he speaks Yiddish. He is a hard-headed, two-fisted, deep-drinking, humorous, hearty man, without an ounce of social theory in his head but with a very practical realization of the need for change.

In an interview published in "Today" he is quoted as saying, "I have never read a line of Karl Marx or Lenin and it seems to me the Russians have been too drastic and dictatorial in their methods of creating a new social order. But the fact remains that our own system here has broken down. It no longer fits modern conditions. We've got to change the system."

His career reveals him as a man who loves adventure, has never shrunk from dramatic personal changes, and has faced risks. His father was employed in the railway yards at Minneapolis and was correspondingly subject to the scanty pay and lay-offs of the depression period of the '90's. Times were hard for the Olson family and at an early age—thirteen years—young Floyd had to help support the household by newspaper route-work. Then he got a job as a freight trucker with the railway, joined the union, tried to study law but found that the combination of night-work with a course of studies was too much for him. So he set out to see the world.

He saw it. He sold farm machinery in Western Canada, worked a couple of years in Alaska as a miner, a fisherman, a longshoreman and a scow-hand, returning to Minneapolis in 1913, where he got a day job in a law office and attended a night law school. In 1915 he was admitted to the Minneapolis Bar and, after his marriage in 1917, went into State politics, being appointed Assistant County Attorney for Hennepin County in 1919. The following year he was unanimously appointed to the County Attorneyship, a post which he held for ten years, or until his election as the first Farmer-Labor Governor of any state in the Union.

II

His significance in the national scheme of politics rests primarily on the fact that he is a powerful figure in the region which must be held loyal to the New Deal if Roosevelt expects to carry through his policies of reform. There

are, however, additional reasons why Olson must be considered carefully by the White House tacticians.

First, he is one of the two most radical respectable governors in the country—the other being Phil LaFollette.

Second, the Farmer-Labor Party is the one "Third
Party" movement which is well-established and can
serve as rallying ground for the left-wingers. It is not a
flash in the pan like current depression panaceas, nor yet
an untried force. It kept alive during the big post-war
prosperity wave and developed rapidly as the depression
wore on. In the 1934 elections there were Farmer-Labor
movements in several States, including Oregon, and
though none of these movements was especially strong
they were all symptomatic of an ominous chemical change
in the attitude of the electorate. Through the League for
Independent Political Action, moreover, the party maintained a national alliance, reaching into the East. Howard
Y. Williams, former executive secretary of the League—
John Dewey is its chairman—became head of the Farmer-
Labor Political Federation and presided over the Minnesota State Convention of 1934, at which a politically
embarrassing radical program was adopted. The Farmer-
Labor Political Federation is actively at work trying to
unite the various leaders of discontent behind a single
leader. Olson is their candidate. And Olson, running on
a platform like the 1934 platform of his party in Minnesota, might well obtain the support of the Socialist Party,
as indicated by Norman Thomas's letter published in
"The New York Herald-Tribune" on April 2, 1935.

Third, the Party has put forward elements of a national
program in Congress, through Representative Lundeen,
a Farmer-Laborite, who is sponsor of the Lundeen Unemployment Insurance Bill, a measure which has the

backing of nearly all the aggressive labor and radical groups. The Farmer-Laborites in Congress are the nucleus of the newly-formed "progressive bloc" of about fifty Representatives, who have agreed to support a number of measures somewhat more radical than those officially sponsored by the New Deal Administration.

Fourth, Olson is respectable—radical but respectable. People aren't investigating his income tax returns nor would they find anything if they did.

Fifth, Olson has had actual administrative experience and is a very practical politician.

Sixth, Olson represents a party with a reasonably well-rounded platform instead of a few catchwords or phrases. Much of the Farmer-Labor platform is incorporated in Coughlin's platform for his National Union for Social Justice. Farmer-Labor leaders in the agrarian States have been talking in a complimentary way about Coughlin for President in 1936. Olson is much more likely than Long is to attract liberal Catholic support.

The Farmer-Labor program in fact is a very well-considered device—politically speaking—to provide common ground for the various currents of dissent in the Mississippi Valley region. It includes an EPIC plank—now in actual operation—for the State to take over idle factories, operate them by the unemployed and distribute the products to the needy; a mortgage moratorium law which was sustained by the Supreme Court; a Huey Long exemption of homesteads valued up to $4,000 from taxation; a LaFollette increase in graduated taxes on large incomes, gifts and inheritances; a central state reserve bank owned entirely by the State; an Ickes law to permit cities, towns and villages to own, operate and sell current from power and light plants; a Huey Long proposal for free text books; and the usual provisions for unemployment, sickness, accident and workmen's compensation insurance, maternity benefits and an "adequate old age pension."

One of the notable things about this program is that it avoids the monetary panaceas, so popular among certain groups which prefer inflation to reform. The other notable thing is that, while it offers itself as the protector of the small business man, it has thrown overboard the old trust-busting attitude. Instead of following Brandeis in denouncing the "curse of bigness," it proposes the nationalization or coöperativization of the big industries. It proposes trust-busting only when the big fellows compete with the little fellows and boasts that Minnesota has a higher chain-store tax than any other State.

The Farmer-Labor crowd stresses the coöperative element, probably because of the Scandinavian tradition of coöperation which has been transplanted to Minnesota. The platform of the Party would, in fact, be regarded as mild and reasonable in the consumer-economy country of Sweden. At the same time, the Farmer-Labor leaders feel compelled to play down the element of socialization and nationalization, and the "radical" 1934 platform caused Olson and the Party to lose ground with the more conservative Scandinavian voters of Minnesota.

The preamble to this platform said: "Palliative measures will continue to fail. Only a complete reorganization of the present social structure into a coöperative commonwealth will bring economic security and prevent a prolonged period of suffering among the people. We therefore declare that capitalism has failed and that immediate steps must be taken by the people to abolish capitalism in a peaceful and lawful manner, and that a new, sane, and just society must be established; a system in which all the natural resources, machinery of production, transportation, and communication shall be owned by the government and operated democratically for the benefit of all the people and not for the benefit of the few."

Olson happened to be in Washington—as was the Farmer-Labor Senator Shipstead—at the time the platform committee, largely influenced by Eastern doctrinaire radicals, did its work. Despite vigorous opposition from veteran Farmer-Laborites, the platform was put over and Olson accepted it, but, as the summer wore on, the Party decided to suppress it. The Republicans and Democrats cited this preamble as a means of frightening the little business men and the farmers, so the Party felt compelled to get out an official circular of explanation and, with typical shrewdness, circulated the explanation but not the platform.

In this connection, it is important to note that the Farmer-Labor Party is a Party—in the accepted meaning —far more than it is a program. In other words, it represents the interests and views of a large body of men, and develops its proposals as it goes along, just like the other parties. For the Farmer-Labor Party grew out of the old Non-Partisan League movement in the Dakotas, as a combination of the mine and railroad workers and the farmers. Henrik Shipstead, the Farmer-Labor Senator whom one of the Hoover Administration tellingly compared to a large, nice Newfoundland dog where economics were concerned, was the League's candidate for Congressman in 1918, but was defeated. In 1920, he ran for Governor of Minnesota, and was again defeated. But the 1922 "swing-back" from the Harding "normalcy" victory of 1920, combined with the post-war slump in farm prices, sent Shipstead to the U. S. Senate, where he was joined a year later by Magnus Johnson. Both men ran under the new Farmer-Labor label.

This was the peak of the Farmer-Labor movement until

the great depression began eating into traditional party lines—although it joined in the Third Party movement of 1924 which was led by the elder LaFollette.

While Olson was serving as County Attorney of Hennepin County, which contains the city of Minneapolis, he joined the Farmer-Labor group. His prosecuting career was vigorous and he took a flyer for the Governorship in 1924, but was beaten. He did not try again until 1930, when he was elected Governor with the help of a Democratic alliance. He was reëlected in 1932 and again in 1934 when, as a result of the "radical" platform, he made a relatively poor showing, running 35,000 votes behind Shipstead.

This was also due to the truckmen's strike of the summer of 1934, when he was caught between the extremely reactionary Citizens' Alliance, with which he had fought before, and the increasingly radical and grim truckmen. The Citizens' Alliance had made Minneapolis, with Los Angeles, one of the two great "open shop" cities of America, and during the strike one of its officials protested to a large hospital in Minneapolis that it should make a rule not to accept wounded strikers. Olson finally declared martial law—the first time martial law had been declared to protect strikers in America—but the Communist groups, which had been making headway while the sun shone, denounced his action as a "Fascist strike-breaking move." For a time it looked as though this would cause Olson to lose the support of the more radical labor groups but, after the strike had subsided, when the election was held, he kept his labor vote reasonably well but lost among the more conservative Scandinavian farmers.

Olson is a red-headed, large-boned, big-chested, boyish-looking man, with a friendly but forceful personality. He prides himself on being a "practical" politician and on scorning political bunk. None of the political visiting firemen who descend on Washington talks to newspaper men with greater frankness, and he has the slightly cynical, direct manner that they like. After the campaign of 1934 he was asked by a group of Washington correspondents why he played down the radical program his Party had adopted in the spring.

"Because it scared the devil out of Minnesota," was his reply, slightly paraphrased.

He is a gusty liver—as hearty in his way as Roosevelt— who can take and hold his liquor in competition with the best of them and who exerts a powerful influence on women who respond to strength and vitality. He is perfectly at home in a full-dress suit but wears it as though he were just a little contemptuous of it, and, like many leaders of the "underdog," he rather enjoys annoying people who attach importance to social conventions.

For example, in the spring of 1932, when the Governors' Conference was held in Richmond, Virginia, President Hoover invited all the Governors to dine with him at the White House the evening after the conference ended. Everyone showed up but Olson. The Governors were kept herded in line by the White House ushers—the mechanics of entertaining reached their highest point of engineering efficiency under the Hoovers—for about half an hour, while ushers, police and a battery of telephone operators tried to locate the contrary-minded Viking from Minneapolis. He was finally located, out spending the evening with some political and newspaper friends, with whom he continued to spend the evening, saying that he had wired declining the White House invitation—itself a thing "not done"—the day before. The telegraphic refusal was somehow never located by the White House social secretariat.

With the help of Burt Wheeler, Roosevelt took Olson into camp in 1932. Before his nomination for the Presidency, F.D.R. went to Minneapolis in the spring of that year and sounded a call to arms in the farm belt. He paid a long visit to Olson's office and lavished praise on him in his speech. As a matter of fact, the wing of the Democratic Party which then controlled what was left of the party machinery in Minnesota was in alliance with the Farmer-Labor crowd and was conducting a bitter fight with the Irish Catholic group in St. Paul, who came out for Al Smith as against Roosevelt in 1932 and got partial control of the Party machinery in 1934. Olson tagged along with Roosevelt in 1932 and has been pretty friendly with him ever since.

In 1934, Roosevelt again tried to keep the Farmer-Labor people in line for the New Deal, by giving Senator Shipstead an audience on his way back to Washington from the Pacific Coast and by patting Olson on the back in passing. Later on, however, "Big Jim" and his statistical wizard, Emil Hurja, went out to Minnesota, were rendered giddy by visions of a straight Democratic victory in a State where the Democrats were the "Third Party," and generally balled things up for the Administration's major strategy. Hurja even went back and delivered a radio speech, bitterly attacking Olson and saying that the "Administration" wanted him and Shipstead defeated. Hurja's charges of improper handling of relief by Olson were quickly refuted by Harry Hopkins, and Louis McHenry Howe had to spend a couple of tortured days cleaning up the mess.

Since then, however, Olson has not changed his tune. With the air of one making positive statements of fact rather than delivering himself of a hope, he says that there will be a Third Party movement in 1936 if Roosevelt goes too conservative but that the big break won't come until 1940 if Roosevelt carries out the liberal promise of the New Deal. Until recently at least, Olson has doubted that 1936 would be the year of victory for a national ticket headed by Olson. Instead, he has plans to run for the Senate. This doesn't mean that Olson would refuse to support a Third Party candidate in 1936. He would probably back Wheeler if the latter should run—but Wheeler won't run unless he can get Farmer-Labor support pledged in advance.

III

For the present, in fact, Olson is distinctly on the defensive. The Farmer-Laborites are in a minority in both of the branches of the State Legislature. Practically none of his program passed this year, and a legislative committee has been appointed to investigate his conduct of the State's departments and of the handling of Minnesota relief.

He is accused of having exacted political tribute from relief workers, as in Ohio and North Dakota, but Hopkins states that there is no reason to investigate. Ickes started an investigation which gathered material to turn over to the Department of Justice, and then announced that the investigation had ceased.

More sobering is the fact that, although he won the 1934 election, it was by considerably less than a 100,000 plurality in a three-cornered fight and that he lost most heavily in the country districts. The Scandinavian farmers are stubborn and don't like to be branded as "Reds" although they are pretty liberal, on the Swedish order of liberalism. Besides, his State tax program is very heavy,

including a new State income tax enacted into law at his
insistence last year.

Recently the Minnesota Republicans have picked up
courage and plan to fight against his Senatorial ambitions
for 1936. For the first time the Republican ex-Governor
Theodore Christianson has not turned a deaf ear to the
suggestion that he go out against Schall, the blind mud-
slinger, in the primary. Olson could beat Schall but is not
certain that he could beat Christianson. At the same time,
Olson's relations with other radical candidates are not
discreet. Huey Long is reported to have sent an emissary
to Olson about the same time the Kingfish approached
Coughlin, but Olson turned him down, saying that he
had ambitions of his own. Moreover, his "practicality"
as a politician has led him to use his office to build up a
personal political machine which distresses the lily-white
reformers.

Olson's judgment of opportunity is excellent and he
possesses personal caution, but he is vulnerable in that
his Farmer-Labor following could be weakened and possibly split by a conservative Republican campaign on the
order of the one devised to beat Upton Sinclair in California. If, as many believe inevitable, the trend of national politics is to accentuate cleavages between the left
and the right, a considerable number of his slow-thinking,
stubborn, conservative farmers will desert him, while the
vote of labor is always, and quite naturally, dictated by
short-range considerations. A man whose living depends
on a weekly pay-envelope cannot indulge the same liberty
of political action which is permitted to a farmer who,
after all, has a house—even if mortgaged—from which he
cannot be easily evicted and who possesses the means to
produce the food and fuel needed for his household.

Olson may be more important to Roosevelt as a weather cock than as an active political power. He is not a national figure—yet. And, if he decides to wait for 1940 to try for the Presidency, he has an important hurdle to clear in the Senatorial election of 1936. He might be licked. It is just possible that if Christianson were to go out for the Republican nomination for Senator, with every prospect of victory, Olson would decide to take a gamble on a Third Party national ticket. If he ran for the Senate, however, he would be in the market for a coalition with the Democrats—in which case he would probably do better by refraining from attacking Roosevelt. Olson, in his attitude toward the New Deal, is likely to be a fairly accurate barometer of the state of mind of those people in the North Central States whose votes can make and break presidents, parties, and administrations. As a Presidential candidate, he would lack the liabilities of Long and Coughlin, while he might well reap the benefits of their support.

VI

THE ROVER BOYS AT ARMAGEDDON

GIVEN A SITUATION in which there is a constant demand for at least one good deed a day, the Boy Scout is at a premium in American politics. Where a man like Assistant Secretary of State Francis B. Sayre wears his frat pin on his diplomatic pyjamas, and Phi Beta Kappa supplies the keys to the city of Washington, there must be men who will go on political hikes with F.D.R. and light a fire with one match at the end of the trail.

Such are the LaFollettes of Wisconsin in our present contact with the foes of the Lord at Armageddon. They are pivot men in politics, sitting securely on the hinges which link the swaying left-wingers with the stable Easterners. If there is something wide-eyed and glad-handed about the LaFollette technique it has not prevented them from staking their claim to the precise spot at which the New Deal intersects with the Western revolt. They are the only men who can make the New Deal seem revolutionary to the Westerners and they are the only men who can make revolution seem respectable to the New Dealers. They may possess the wisdom of the dove but theirs is also the innocence of the serpent. After all, in the books, the aboriginal Rover Boys invariably worsted the bully and came out on top of the pile.

Theirs is the perennial youth of juvenile thrillers— the only authentic political dynasty in modern America.

Theirs is also the morale which goes with adherence to a single political creed—the Wisconsin Idea. This was the life-work of their father—"Old Bob" LaFollette—who emerged from the trust-busting and rail-baiting of the Granger revolt of the '90's as Governor of Wisconsin in 1900. His creed was simple: that "the will of the people shall be the law of the land" and that economic democracy is attainable by political means. The means which he devised for Wisconsin made the State University a sort of service station for scientific administration. In 1906, he moved on to the United States Senate, where he remained until his death in 1925, fighting the "interests" year in and year out. He held aloof from Teddy's Progressive revolt in 1912 but led another himself in 1924, as a means of advertising the persistence of the Wisconsin Idea in darkest normalcy. His death left both the Idea and the LaFollette dynasty securely established in the north-central region of the United States and in the American tradition of politics.

For some thirty years, Wisconsin has been the most progressive State in the Union and has spread the fame of the LaFollettes throughout the English-speaking and democratic world. Under the leadership of the LaFollettes, Wisconsin has been the nation's legislative proving ground. The erstwhile "radicalism" of the elder LaFollette is the orthodox Republicanism of to-day. This has been the normal course of procedure: First, some "lunatic fringe" group or party proposes; second, the LaFollettes take it up and try it out in Wisconsin; third, in due course of time, the nation follows, after denouncing the Lafollettes as dangerous innovators.

As a result, there is nothing of a fly-by-night character in the LaFollette tradition and the Wisconsin Idea, nothing demagogic, nothing Fascistic. Where Huey Long will have to disinfect himself with the radicals and where Olson will have to prove the staying power of the Farmer-Labor movement, the LaFollettes are dealing with a tested and acceptable political force. As a matter of fact, the LaFollette tradition in Wisconsin has been stabler, more constant, than the tradition of either major party. The Democratic Party could nominate a John W. Davis in 1924 and a Franklin D. Roosevelt in 1932, and still remain the Democratic Party. The Republicans could skip from a Theodore Roosevelt to a Warren G. Harding, and from a Coolidge to a Hoover, and still be Republican, but the Wisconsin Idea remains, after thirty years, still the Wisconsin Idea—not a static program but a theory of progress through democratic processes, not a day-dream but a series of concrete achievements. The LaFollette tradition has become so much a part of American political folk-lore that its disappearance would be like the end of the passenger pigeons or the clipper ships.

While everybody has been talking about forming a Third Party, the LaFollettes have been doing something about it. They formed one in 1934, and for purely practical reasons. They were not sure they could win in the Republican primary, because so many of their old followers had been won over to the Democratic Party. They were not sure they could win in the Democratic primary, because not enough of their followers had swung over. Their best chance was to form a third party which would assure them a place on the final ballot. It was a risk but they won, leaving them in a position to swing the liberal votes of their State in the most effective way, for or against a national Third Party candidate.

They have not swung so far to the left as did Olson and the Farmer-Laborites in 1934; perhaps they were wise, for the Farmer-Labor group swung a little too far and had to back-track. Nevertheless, it has left Olson in a position to make a bid for national Third Party leadership, although he might find it difficult to get the Eastern labor support the LaFollettes could command. Phil LaFollette, despite his refusal to take a job under Roosevelt, will have to shift over to the left again in order to differentiate himself from the New Deal. With one member of the family in and one squatting on the borders of the New Deal, the LaFollettes may be in a strategical position but only on the assumption that they are right in playing their game on the theory that the great break-up will come in 1940 at the end of Roosevelt's second term. One of the LaFollettes is much more likely to be nabbed as a Vice-Presidential candidate to make a victory for someone else— the Democratic Party or a Third Party—than to lead the movement. By 1940, one of the two brothers—Phil and Bob—may be strong enough to lead, but Roosevelt could probably run with Bob as a Vice-Presidential candidate without turning in a riot call in 1936. It might offend some of the old-line Southern Democrats but Bob would not alarm the Eastern conservatives more than Roosevelt has already alarmed them. In fact, he might alarm them less, for he is slower, steadier, and stays put, whereas they are never sure what Roosevelt will do next.

This is because Roosevelt has all the privileges of genius, including the right to change his mind, where the LaFollette boys are more concerned with being the heirs of a great tradition than with magnetizing the following which creates traditions, and smashes them.

II

"Young Bob" LaFollette, now aged forty, never wanted to go into politics. He wanted to be a banker. He tried to run away from politics but his father haled him back and held him to the family tradition as though it were a family curse.

Robert Marion LaFollette, Jr.—to give him his correct name—has been in the Senate for almost ten years—and all by accident. When his father died in 1925 the family held a council. Phil, the younger brother, had been regarded as "Old Bob's" logical successor. He had some of the traditional LaFollette flair and personality, where Young Bob was more staid, less dramatic. But Phil was two years under age for the Senate, which threw the choice between Mrs. LaFollette, Sr., and Young Bob, who was a few months beyond the Constitutional minimum age of thirty. He was designated to run, made his campaign and was elected to complete his father's term. In 1928, year of the Hoover landslide, he was renominated and re-elected. And, in 1934, as the candidate of the new Progressive Party, he was elected once again—this time in a three-cornered fight against the Tory Republicans and the Old Deal Democrats.

Few men have had a better training for service in the Senate than Young Bob. As a boy he imbibed the atmosphere and talk of the Wisconsin Idea in the Governor's mansion at Madison. When his father came to Washington, Bob spent most of his spare time watching the Senate in session, listening to his father. He attended the University of Wisconsin for a time but was forced to discontinue his college course on account of illness. When he returned to Washington, his father was just entering the worst of his periods of ostracism because of his futile efforts to keep the United States out of the World War. These efforts were accompanied by flaming speeches which stand out as prophecies in the cold gray light of the Nineteen Thirties. What LaFollette, Lindbergh (the pacifist father of the flying colonel who married the daughter of a Morgan partner), Norris and a few others saw then is now generally realized and is the main driving force behind the movement to assure American isolation by bans on loans to nations at war, embargoes on the export of munitions, and revision of American policy so as to substitute neutrality for "friendly neutrality."

At the time, LaFollette was branded as "pro-German" and cries arose for his expulsion from the Senate. Just then Young Bob became critically ill with pneumonia and for weeks the old Senator spent most of his time at his eldest son's bedside, snatching sleep when he could on a cot in the same room. When Young Bob pulled through, the old man made him his secretary and there the boy remained for six years. His duties were largely political and he served for a time as chairman of the Wisconsin State Republican Committee. During his father's campaign tours, he talked to the politicians while his brother Phil practiced speaking to the crowds. In 1924, he was vice-chairman of his father's campaign for the Presidency on a third-party ticket, and learned some of the statutory pitfalls by which entrenched State political machines have rendered a new party movement virtually illegal—a consideration which is shaping his course to-day.

Then, in 1925, he succeeded to his father's seat in the Senate, virtually by inheritance—an interesting commentary on the validity of the democratic principle for which his father fought. Slight of figure, with plastered-down black hair, short and direct in manner, Young Bob is a sober, undramatic figure in comparison with his father. His speeches are not exhilarating, although they are as full of meat as a cocoanut. He seldom speaks until he has mastered his subject and few men in the Senate are more intelligent students of public affairs.

Yet even though the tradition of personality is somewhat diluted, the tradition of the Wisconsin Idea is carried on in full force by Young Bob. For ten years, George Norris has looked upon him with dim and fatherly eyes as the great Progressive hope for the future, and he has given the Republican Party plenty of opportunity to speculate on the persistence of the Progressive spirit. In the Republican National Convention of 1928—that bossed and bewildered assemblage which was responsible for inflicting Hoover on the nation—Young Bob arose, as his father had done at convention after convention, to present the Wisconsin program and to protest against the majority recommendations of the platform committee. At first he received a few of the jeers and hisses which had regularly greeted his father but when, after reading his minority report, he reminded the convention that thirty-two out of the thirty-five planks presented to the convention of 1908 by his father, twenty years before, had become law, he gave the Republicans something to think about. They applauded him when he finished with a heartiness which was a novelty to a LaFollette from such a gathering.

Until the depression, Young Bob's Senate accomplishments were nothing to write home about. He voted with the agrarians and other progressives on most questions. In 1929 he was one of the leaders of the Progressive-Democratic coalition against the Hawley-Smoot tariff in its original horrible form, although the final law was nothing to view with pride. Among his chief exploits was the abolition of secret Senate sessions to consider executive appointments. Among his other projects were an investigation of labor troubles in the anthracite region, a resolution to prevent the use of Federal Reserve credit for speculative purposes, and a resolution to study the extent of unemployment and ways of relieving it.

His real chance came with the depression, which he rightly regarded as a challenge to democracy and not as an interesting problem in financial manipulation. He stepped to the front at once with an investigation of its causes and cures and his plan for setting up an economic council—later partially realized through the N.R.A. and the A.A.A. With Wagner and Costigan, he was first in the Senate to arrive at an intelligent diagnosis of the depression and the first to present means of combating it. With those two Senators, he led the fight for unemployment insurance, for a large public works program and for Federal relief to the unemployed.

It was significant that he was more active in his studies and proposals for dealing with the industrial end of the depression than with the agricultural end. The agricultural program advanced by the Western farm leaders to deal with the post-war depression was pretty well-established when he arrived in the Senate, and he supported it, despite its inherent inconsistency as a program for subsidized dumping on the theory that it would benefit us to export surplus farm products without reference to imports. He saw what the majority of the farm leaders did not see, that the solution to the major problem lay in industry and finance. Under his guidance, the La-Follette program once again became—or remained—a national, not a sectional, program.

In 1932, following the example of George Norris, the LaFollettes supported Roosevelt and Young Bob was called into Roosevelt's councils to help with the unemployment relief and public works bills. On the whole he has supported the New Deal, and his variations naturally

have been to the left. He fought unsuccessfully for larger
public works appropriations. He, Costigan and Wagner
wanted five billion dollars or more in 1933 instead of $3,-
3c0,000,000; they wanted eight instead of four billion in
1935. He never loses an opportunity to propose higher income and inheritance taxes—though nothing really confiscatory, as proposed by Long—but has shown lamentably
little interest in proposals designed to alter the administration of the income tax laws so as to make them less exas-
perating to the people in the middle brackets.

Roosevelt has teamed consistently with the LaFollettes
—he'd better, as they represent his real grip on the Middle
West—and in 1934, after they formed their third party,
he went to Green Bay to make a speech which would help
Young Bob. He gave Bob a big smile and mentioned his
name in a pleasant manner—which was meant to con-
stitute an endorsement—but at the same time he took a
veiled crack at Phil, running for Governor, who had refused to be lured into taking a job under the New Deal.
However, the crack was generally thought to be aimed at
Borah, who was then much more in the public eye, so no
harm was done. Finally, on the eve of election, Roosevelt
telegraphed Bob to come and see him immediately after
the votes were counted, an invitation that Bob used,
with the permission of the White House, to wind up his
campaign. Both the LaFollettes were triumphantly elected
in Wisconsin—Phil for Governor, Bob for Senator—which
suggests that Roosevelt needs the LaFollettes more than
they need him.

Bob came to the white House *ventre à terre,* and was let
in on the $4,880,000,000 work relief program, then being
hammered into shape. Both the program and the invitation tickled him; he has been privy to Roosevelt's outline of his plans for the future of the New Deal (and it

would sound pretty grand to any liberal), so Bob has remained loyal to F.D.R. When Burt Wheeler broached the subject of forming a progressive bloc to work toward the formation of a third party, Bob replied that he thought that the time wasn't ripe yet, that Roosevelt "still has several rabbits in his hat." Bob voted for the McCarran amendment which tied up the big work relief bill, but when the issue came up again, he voted the other way, explaining that while he thought prevailing wage rates ought to be paid, the most important thing was to get the money appropriated for work, and that some of those who voted for prevailing wages were in fact trying to knock work out altogether and force the appropriation down to a mere dole.

That is the measure of Bob. He is a practical politician who has very little personal ambition. So far as he is concerned, the New Deal has caught up with the Wisconsin Idea, and Bob has not moved fast enough to keep from being overhauled. Like Norris, he will stand up for his principles and deal a blow for them when he thinks it will be effective, but will go along with Roosevelt so long as Roosevelt is liberal. If it comported with his principles to play the Wheeler and Long game of keeping out in front, he is smart enough to do it, but he is too intelligent, too conscientious, to support a man like Long, and is far from convinced that Wheeler, who conceals his Socialist principles under the motley of Free Silver and Prairie Trust-Busting, is the answer to the national riddle.

He trains along with Roosevelt, *faute de mieux,* and, as one cynical liberal put it: "Franklin D. is going to be too smart for Young Bob."

III

As a matter of fact, Bob was never considered the brainy
one of the family. Phil LaFollette, now thirty-eight, was
always the white-haired boy of the LaFollettes. He was
to inherit the crown. Good old Bob was the plodding,
dependable one. Bob went through college creditably
enough but Phil's record at the University of Wisconsin
was positively brilliant, and he was the dynamic member
of the family who was designed to succeed his father in
the United States Senate. But the elder LaFollette died
in 1925, when Phil was too young to take a Senatorial seat
legally, and the dynasty had to be represented at Washington by Bob.

Phil is a dramatic "chip off the old block" where Bob
is a refined splinter. Phil has short, bushy hair in typical
LaFollette pompadour style, where Bob's is slicked back.
He is fiery, impassioned, like his father, whereas Bob is
more sober and informative. Phil was an honor student
in the University of Wisconsin and in its law school, where
he subsequently taught; Bob got along all right but had
neither the outstanding scholastic nor the personal abilities of his brother. Phil is political paprika; Bob is the
salt of the earth, and human nature being what it is, the
majority of people get along better with Bob and his
policies while they have greater enthusiasm for Phil and
his ambitions.

Phil campaigned with his father in 1924, when he was
twenty-seven years old. Since it had been impossible for
Phil to run for the Senate after his father's death, and
since Wisconsin would probably not cherish two La-
Follette Senators, if only to avoid confusion, it was finally
decided that Phil should run for Governor in 1930. He
did, and was nominated in opposition to Governor Kohler

by 100,000 votes. Formerly, like his father, he had been the District Attorney of Dane County, in which capacity he had been amiable and conscientious—characteristics which mark his official personality as Governor. In 1928 Hoover carried Wisconsin by 90,000 votes, and Phil ridiculed him unmercifully in the 1930 campaign. Phil won by a hundred thousand. Since his election, voices have been raised protesting against this family monopoly of high office, to which "The Progressive"—the family pep sheet—has replied that nobody criticizes the Mayo Brothers for running a clinic. And nobody criticizes the Marx Brothers for staging their act, either. As a matter of fact, Wisconsin likes the LaFollette act, on the whole, and doesn't object to the family half-nelson on the Wisconsin Idea.

In his first term as Governor, at the age of thirty-three, Phil had control of the Assembly (the lower house in the Wisconsin State Legislature) and held fifteen Progressive seats in the Senate against the sixteen of the opposition, with two independents holding the balance of power. Phil LaFollette may be credited with the first State "Brain Trust," for, as a youthful Governor, he did not hesitate to bring expert help in from the outside. For example, he named as chairman of the Wisconsin Railroad Commission, David Lilienthal, now on the Tennessee Valley Authority.

As a youthful Governor, Phil proposed several enterprises during the 1931–33 term, which sound remarkably like New Deal propositions. For instance, he suggested that unemployed, unmarried men be put in scarlet mackinaws with corduroy trousers and hip boots and sent to winter cantonments where courses in adult education would be available. In summer they were to reforest the areas which the Wisconsin lumber barons had denuded.

This plan was never undertaken—possibly because of the scarlet mackinaws in a State which still responds to Hearstian yammerings about "reds" and "radicals." Phil's public works project to eliminate grade crossings raised the gasoline tax from two to four cents a gallon but only 6,071 men were employed for an average of seven weeks during the first year of its operation—a lesson which might well have been called to the attention of the New Dealers in 1933.

During his first term, Phil did eliminate the State tax on real estate, which was a great help to farmers already burdened with local taxes, and he persuaded most of the counties to suspend the sale of farms for delinquent taxes. Moreover, the "waiver plan" of his State Banking Department saved many banks from failure. The thing which probably beat him in the 1932 Republican primary for the Governorship was his proposed income tax law by which a State tax started at 1 per cent for corporation and private incomes and ascended progressively—in the manner dear to progressives—to 30 per cent on incomes over $100,000, with all dividends taxable and no capital losses deductible. This income tax reform was eventually adopted, in a milder form, with the elimination of the surtaxes on high incomes. For some reason, Progressives seem unable to get away from the notion that the purpose of taxation is to punish people for having taxable incomes instead of raising revenue—a fact which generally leads to their overthrow before they have accomplished the social purposes for which they levy the taxes. For the object of their social policy should be to eliminate rather than to tax the high incomes which are symptoms of inequitable economic institutions.

In his first campaign, Phil emphasized the necessity of unemployment insurance and a rather clumsy law for that purpose was passed, although its application was delayed until 1935. Phil lost out in 1932, however, although he voluntarily reduced his salary as Governor from $7,500 to $6,000. In that year, the Democratic landslide, abetted by the LaFollettes, carried Schmedeman into the office of Governor, as a New Deal Democrat. As seems to be conventional in such cases, he promptly became considerably more conservative than the "Stalwart" Republicans whom the LaFollettes had fought for a generation. Phil took the opportunity of making a trip abroad, including a visit to Russia, and was offered, according to a public statement by his brother Bob, eight important Federal posts and refused them all.

In 1934, Phil decided to tackle the Governorship again, and he was elected, despite New Deal support for Schmedeman. His Legislature is opposed to him, although he actually controls the lower house through an alliance of Progressives plus liberal Democratic Roosevelt legislators against the Republicans, and elected a Progressive Chairman. In the Senate, there is a lineup of fourteen Democrats, thirteen Progressives and six Republicans. The April, 1935, elections to fill two vacancies in the Senate were a decided victory for the LaFollettes, as both seats were filled by Progressives.

Phil put over the State Relief Bill, with the State matching Federal funds by $10,000,000. This bill provides for a special tax on telephone companies in Wisconsin and was partially vetoed by LaFollette, an action which is now before the State Supreme Court for a decision as to its legality.

Philip LaFollette has more ability, more charm, more fire than his brother Bob. He is a better speaker and votegetter. While Bob makes advances to the Roosevelt Administration, Phil stands on his own ideas, concurring when he agrees with the Federal Administration, and boldly dissenting when he is in fundamental disagreement.

Yet Bob is right and Phil is wrong, for the truth of the matter is that the New Deal has caught up with the La-Follettes, in the sense that there is not much more left that States can do as individual sovereignties. States are rapidly declining in importance and since the F.E.R.A. and P.W.A. were established they are tending to become administrative subdivisions of the central government instead of free and equal elements in a federation. The only major measures which can bring results are national measures.

Thus Governorships no longer provide the opportunities for demonstrative action that they did at the time when the elder LaFollette devised the Wisconsin Idea. We are rapidly on our way to the condition where States will be only provinces, so far as concerns economic legislation. The Federal Government must set the pace, using bribes and threats and tax measures to assure State cooperation. In cultural and police matters, the States can be as individualistic as they like, but the day of the State reformer—the day to which Justice Brandeis and old-fashioned progressives of his school try to turn back the hands of the clock—is gone forever.

We have become a national entity in economic matters and in future no State—not even Wisconsin—can be a proving ground for national experiments of any importance much longer. A State party like the Wisconsin Progressives—a third party with state control—can advocate certain reforms, certain changes, certain methods. It can advocate nationalization of coal mines or all utilities, or nationalization of anything else, but it is powerless to do much inside the realm of the State. For this reason, it should be noted that the LaFollette State Progressive program of 1934 is a national program, and coincides very closely with the policies of the New Deal.

Its chief points of divergence are to the left of the New Deal—but not very far to the left—and in the main it is a straight, old-fashioned liberal program for the nation and *not* for the State of Wisconsin. The extent of its "radicalism" shows that it is still very close to the New Deal, as its planks include the following proposals:

(1) That the distribution of milk should be declared a public utility (and a good many of Roosevelt's closest friends and advisers think the same);

(2) That there should be a government-owned central bank (and that is what the New Deal is driving toward with Eccles as Governor of the Federal Reserve Board);

(3) That there should be prompt payment of the soldiers' bonus (a good vote-catching device, which happens to coincide roughly with the Administration belief that the main solution of the depression will come through redistributing purchasing power);

(4) That the manufacture and sales of munitions of war should be nationalized (another good vote-catcher to which the New Deal is not unfriendly but which ignores the fact that the munitions industry cannot be segregated from the peace-time chemical industry).

The importance of this program—and the significance of the two young hopefuls who drafted it and who represent the Progressive Party in State and National politics —is the fact that it offers the bridge over which the Democrats of the East and South must pass, to join forces—or do battle—with the farm radicals of the Prairie States. For Wisconsin is a key State in the New Deal's struggle to hold the farm belt. If the LaFollettes go with Roosevelt they cannot assure a New Deal victory in the Middle West, but if they go against him, they can assure the New Deal's defeat in its effort to shape a social and economic policy which will be sufficiently radical to command the support of the discontented farmers of the corn and wheat country.

VII

ONE-TO-SIXTEEN!

THE VARIOUS LINES OF DISSENT from the more conservative phases of the New Deal program would not be particularly important if they could be kept divided and out of focus. Southern California's "Plans"; the Leagues and Unions of the Mississippi Valley, North and South; the "funny money" people and the peasant and proletarian revolts do not particularly matter so long as they find no common meeting-point. Yet, politics being what it is— the science of relativity in human affairs—there must be at least one man who occupies a position which is geographically and emotionally central to all of the left wing turmoil. There is such a man. The odds are strongly against him, as yet, but as an outside chance he cannot be ignored by any competent political book-maker.

Burton Kendall Wheeler, U. S. Senator from the sovereign State of Montana, is the man whom the inner circle of Administration political sleuths has been watching with especial care for the last several months. This is because Wheeler, being "safe" in his own State, can afford to run the risks of the profession of long-range political weather forecaster. His prophecies are not always accurate and when he hoists the cyclone signals, only a spring shower or a local thunder storm may follow. His particular importance lies in the fact that he hoists his signals early— he was for Roosevelt for President before the latter's re-election to the New York Governorship in 1930—while others are still arguing over the portents or tapping the barometer.

"Burt" Wheeler—being a New Englander by birth— has far too much sense to represent a "movement." He prefers availability to popularity and has no great personal following, although he made himself a national figure by his exposure of Harry Daugherty's Department of Justice in 1924, by his smashing of the Ohio Gang which was still firmly in the saddle during Coolidge's first year in the White House, and by his campaign for the Vice-Presidency on the Progressive ticket with the late "Fighting Bob" LaFollette, father of the present Senator. His trips to the Soviet Union, at a time when conservative American opinion regarded Bolshevism as being as contagious as the mumps (unless you were an engineer on a lucrative Soviet contract), also won him the sympathy of large radical groups but he made no particular effort to hold together any considerable organization. Instead, today he has maneuvered himself into the position of an extremely "available" candidate, around whom the various left wingers can rally without feeling that they are submitting to domination or surrendering their individual principles. He is a "dark horse" rather than a "favorite son" for the liberal-plus groups and holds almost the position of an honest broker for the several secessionist movements that have either abandoned (or been abandoned by) Roosevelt or that stand ready to leave the New Deal if Roosevelt luffs too far to starboard.

The elements of strength in Wheeler's position are worth the cool-headed consideration that the Administration high political command has given him.

First, he was co-leader of the Progressive revolt of 1924 which polled 5,000,000 votes against two moderately easygoing Conservative candidates in an era of great national prosperity. That five million following can be considered the irreducible minimum of liberal strength—and that many votes are worth gathering in any man's election.

Second, he has a powerful grip on his home State of Montana and considerable personal prestige in the other northwestern and Rocky Mountain States. This means that he can afford to take chances in national politics, secure in the knowledge that he can't be beaten on his home-grounds, and can, moreover, deliver a fair number of electoral votes from the sparsely populated bailiwicks of the West—and electoral and not popular votes are what count in a national election.

Third, he is a Democratic Progressive and hence a somewhat greater threat to Roosevelt than a Republic Progressive would be. His Presidential candidacy would represent a split in the President's Party and splits are always unlucky for the splittee.

Fourth, he is closely allied with Olson and the Farmer-Labor crowd and probably has a better chance than any other Democrat to obtain support from them, as well as from the remains of the Non-Partisan League of North Dakota, should he run as a Third Party leader. The Administration's strategy depends on holding the Northern Mississippi Valley States in line for the New Deal, but Wheeler could menace its success in such a policy.

Fifth, he is an ardent and emotional believer in the free and unlimited coinage of silver, a policy which appeals strongly to the old Bryan wing of the Democratic Party as well as to such monetary inflationists as Senator Elmer Thomas of Oklahoma and others who believe that high money prices will help the farmer, no matter how such prices are obtained.

Sixth, his monetary policy carries him very close to

Father Coughlin. In fact, Wheeler could say "aye" to almost every plank of the latter's National Union for Social Justice and there is some suspicion that he has been one of Coughlin's monetary coaches. Moreover, Wheeler stands ace-high with the Catholics—the backbone of his support in Montana being Catholic and Montana itself being a strongly Catholic State as a result of the late Jim Hill's land policy for the Northern Pacific (Hill having argued that the Catholics were more docile and orderly, politically and economically, than the Protestants and so, though himself a Protestant, deliberately favored Catholic immigration along the right-of-way of his railroad).

Seventh, Wheeler is very friendly with Huey P. Long, for whom he has acted as guide, interpreter and friend. Excepting Senator Overton of Louisiana and Hattie Caraway of Arkansas—both of whom owe their election to Long—Wheeler is Long's closest buddy in the Senate, lending Long friendly assistance without permitting him to exercise any control. When Huey failed to turn up for the opening of the 1935 session of Congress, he wired Wheeler a message of explanation, promising that he would have an important utterance to deliver as soon as he arrived, and Wheeler read the telegram to the Senate.

Eighth, his association with the elder LaFollette in the 1924 Progressive movement might get Wheeler the support of the Wisconsin Progressives, who have so far played ball with Roosevelt, as well as of George Norris of Nebraska, whose support proved important to Roosevelt in 1932.

Ninth, he was one of the key men in the campaign to nominate Roosevelt in 1932—unlike Long, who did not jump on the bandwagon until he saw that the Roosevelt forces were going to have a majority of the convention and could seat or unseat Long's contested delegation from Louisiana—so Wheeler's secession from the New Deal would have an important psychological back-kick in Roosevelt circles.

Tenth, he has been critical of the N.R.A. and the A.A.A. and might expect to cash in on the trust-busting hankering of small business men and on the farmer's lust to curb the middle-man and processor. If the Republicans put up an Eastern Tory or Herbert Hoover again, Wheeler might get the help of Progressive Republicans like Nye and Borah.

Eleventh, he is one of the most effective stump-speakers in the country, and after all oratory is still the basis of politics in a democracy.

To summarize: Wheeler possesses the apparatus for a hook-up of some kind with most of the actual or potential deserters from the Roosevelt camp. In addition to this fact, he is "respectable," impeccably so. Huey Long has openly talked of running Wheeler for President, realizing that the Senior Senator from Montana would have fewer liabilities than the Voice of the Cane-Brakes and in the belief that Huey could deliver his own strength to Wheeler. There has also been talk of a Long-Wheeler ticket, but Burt is not the man to take second place again on a Third Party ticket with anybody. Wheeler has so far not given any indication of how he will play his hand. He has hung back, maneuvering for position but avoiding the front-line trenches. He is probably playing for 1940—the *annus mirabilis* of American politics—but if 1936 looks like a good gamble for a man with nothing to lose, look out! His past political record shows that he has dramatic abilities which might make history if he decides to employ them to break down Roosevelt.

II

Wheeler is a Massachusetts Quaker by birth. The youngest of ten children, he was born on February 27, 1882—just four weeks after F.D.R. was born, an only child, at fashionable Hyde Park on the Hudson—in the little manufacturing town of Hudson, Massachusetts, only a few miles from Groton, where F.D.R. went to school. Burt attended the Hudson High School and a business college and, after working as a stenographer for a short time in Boston, he attended the University of Michigan Law School, from which he graduated in 1905, one year after F.D.R. completed his undergraduate course at Harvard. Wheeler worked his way through law school, waiting on tables, doing stenographic work, and selling medical and cook books in rural Illinois during the summer vacations. On one of his book-peddling expeditions, he met Miss Lulu M. White, at the little town of Albany, Illinois, and in 1907 he went back, married her and took her out to Montana.

The parallelism between his career and that of Roosevelt is worth noting, not for irony or invidious comparison, but as showing the workings of the New England spirit in two men of the same era, one born to a life of wealth from which he revolted, and the other born to a life which must be made for himself. Both are self-made men, in the best sense of the word, and in both of them the tenacity, the pugnacity and the shrewdness of New England are admirably illustrated.

From law school Wheeler went to Butte, Montana, then one of the crudest and least attractive cities of the country. He had been told by physicians that he ought to live in a high, dry climate, to relieve his asthma and to counteract a disposition to tuberculosis. Wheeler didn't

like Butte—very few people do at first blush—and decided
to go on to Spokane, but as he was waiting for a train he
fell into the hands of six card-sharpers in a saloon and
soon found himself minus all of his cash. It did not take
him long to decide that he had been cheated, so he returned suddenly to the saloon and caught the gang dividing up their winnings. He coolly demanded that his
money be returned, telling them that he had influential
friends, and finally bluffed them into giving him back
enough to get to Spokane. In return, they warned him
to leave town on the next train.

This was enough to decide Wheeler to remain where
he was. Out of sheer contrariness, he stayed in Butte, taking a job as stenographer in a law office. With his law
decree from Michigan, he soon began to get Court assignments to defend penniless offenders and so made a reputation as an effective trial lawyer. After a few months, he
went into partnership with another young attorney and
in 1907 was invited into a partnership in a well-established
Butte firm.

His entry into politics was the result of compulsion. Although a Republican by birth, Wheeler had been converted to the Democratic cause by Bryan and free silver
and the sound and fury of the abortive liberal movements
of 1896 and 1900. The Democracy of Silver Bow County,
which contains Butte, was torn into two embittered factions, so Wheeler, being an outsider, was called upon to
act as a sort of neutral chairman at various meetings. In
return, both factions offered him a nomination for the
State Legislature, which he declined. In 1910, he was
again offered the nomination and this time he accepted
it—in the same year when F.D.R. was offered the nomination to the State Senate in New York. Both men were
elected, Wheeler becoming the youngest lawyer in the

Montana Legislature. More partisan squabbles, plus his own reputation, resulted in his selection as chairman of the Judiciary Committee.

This brought him up against the copper interests in a State which had traditionally been run by "copper" and "cattle." Wheeler swiftly became a marked man, as a result of his audacity in proposing bills to close the loopholes by which the Anaconda Copper Company escaped paying damages to its injured workmen. He also voted for Thomas J. Walsh for United States Senator (Senators were still elected by State Legislatures in that period), but Walsh failed to get a majority and it was later Wheeler's vote which elected a conservative Democrat. As a result, Wheeler came out of his first legislative session marked down for destruction by the copper interests—again a curious parallel with Franklin Roosevelt's first year at Albany, when the latter's spectacular fight against "Blue-Eyed Billy" Sheehan's candidacy for the U. S. Senate won F.D.R. the enmity of the railroads, public utility interests and Tammany Hall.

Wheeler's fight for Walsh won him an alliance with that grim and powerful Catholic politician of Montana, who was later to shock the country with the Teapot Dome prosecutions and who was Roosevelt's original selection for the post of Attorney-General in the New Deal Cabinet. The Walsh group wanted Wheeler to run for Attorney-General of Montana in 1912, and Wheeler was not particularly anxious to make the campaign until he heard that the Anaconda Copper Company intended to prevent his nomination anyhow. That made him angry and he entered the convention fight, losing the nomination by one and one-half votes. In the next year, however, President Wilson made him United States Attorney for the Montana District on the recommendation of Walsh, who had just been elected to the Senate at Washington. Wheeler was then thirty-one years old.

He made an active U. S. Attorney, prosecuting various Republicans—and Democrats, including a Democratic State Treasurer and Democratic State Secretary of State —on charges of conspiracy to defraud the State. Wheeler made his real reputation not by his prosecutions but by his refusals to prosecute. He declined to use his office to prosecute strikers, I.W.W.'s and other social nonconformists whom the copper interests regarded as inconvenient. This put him on the spot during the war, when the Department of Justice under A. Mitchell Palmer made an investigation of accusations from the big interests of Montana that Burton K. Wheeler was a "pro-German," and I.W.W., and —later, of course—a Bolshevik—a characteristic sample of the fine art of conservative mud-slinging at those whom conservatives denounce as irresponsible demagogues.

The anti-Wheeler sentiment was whipped up so high that the conservative (copper) wing of the Democratic party was able to exact Wheeler's resignation as their price to support Walsh in 1918. The Wilson Administration offered Wheeler another job—safe, dignified, out-of-the-way—but he preferred to remain in Montana, where he led the fight to override the Legislature's repeal of the State Primary Law—a characteristic repeal designed to hamstring the Non-Partisan League movement, for it seems to be a law of democracy that its institutions are modified or abolished whenever there is serious possibility that the "wrong" people may use them. In return, the Non-Partisan League offered to back Wheeler for Governor in 1920.

He entered the Democratic primary as the liberal candidate, with the backing of the Non-Partisan movement and a Labor League. He was defeated by 40,000 votes after one of the bitterest and most vituperative campaigns ever staged in Montana, at the height of the post-war Red-baiting hysteria in the year of the Wall Street bomb and the Palmer deportations. Two years later, however, Wheeler won the nomination and election to the United States Senate. He arrived in Washington in December, 1923, at the end of an era.

Harding was dead and Coolidge had taken over the liabilities of the Ohio Gang and the pitiful attempt to restore "normalcy" by announcing that it had been restored. With his usual tactlessness, Wheeler ignored the "tradition" that a new Senator shall keep his mouth shut until he has been "educated," and almost at once set out on a scalping-party. Tom Walsh was exposing the oil scandals and another investigation already had uncovered the scandals in the Veterans' Bureau. Harry Daugherty sat placidly in the office of the Attorney-General and Wheeler argued that such scandals could not have developed unless there had been something more than mere negligence in the Government's prosecuting office. There were plenty of ugly rumors but nobody cared to dig up the facts, with Daugherty in control of the secret service and most Senators with something to conceal. Wheeler boldly plunged in and demanded an investigation, especially of the failure of the Department of Justice to enforce the anti-trust laws. He was frustrated, but he returned to the fight. Eventually, he had the nerve to submit a resolution ordering a Senate investigation by a special committee and naming the members of the committee. He was told that this was practically an insult to the presiding officer of the Senate, who always selected the members of special committees. In reply, Wheeler charged that the Republicans were trying to arrange a "whitewash" of Daugherty and forced the investigation. The membership of the committee was named by the Senate as a whole, and Burton K. Wheeler conducted the investigation.

It was an open "fishing-expedition." The resolution passed on February 29, 1924, at a time when Wheeler knew nothing definite about the Department of Justice. He merely had suspicions. One month later, Wheeler had broken into such a nest of stinking scandals that President Coolidge asked for Daugherty's resignation. Wheeler gave the nation such unforgettable and lurid elements in its politicana as "The Little Green House on K. Street," the amazing saga of Jess Smith, the fixer, who died in such a mysterious manner, and the sensational testimony of Roxie Stinson, Jess' divorced wife. It was Wheeler who exposed the worst cesspools in the political underworld of the Harding régime and gave the background for one of our few good political novels: Samuel Hopkins Adams' "Revelry."

The Department of Justice fought back in the traditional manner of a shaky government, not by defense and house-cleaning but by an attempt to get something on its accuser. Wheeler's past in Montana was carefully raked by a gang of Department of Justice agents, and he was indicted on the charge of using his Senatorial influence to fix up some illegal oil leases for a client. A Senate committee, under the chairmanship of Borah, promptly investigated the charge and completely exonerated Wheeler. It was a year before Wheeler could get the case to trial in Montana—an interesting example of the use of the law's delays for political blackmail, that being the year when Wheeler ran on the Progressive ticket—and was acquitted by the jury in ten minutes. The Department of Justice obtained a second indictment for the same offense in the

District of Columbia, but in December, 1925, the Court dismissed the charge.

With this experience, it is easy to understand why Wheeler may feel some sympathy for Huey Long, who for more than two years has been the subject of investigation by the largest and most relentless corps of agents the Bureau of Internal Revenue has set on the heels of anybody since Capone. Long's effort to get a Senate investigation of Jim Farley was patterned on Wheeler's drive on the Department of Justice, though Big Jim is no Harry Daugherty. It is Huey's way of trying to make the income tax investigation look purely political.

The capstone of Wheeler's sensational rise to national prominence in the spring of 1924 was his nomination on the Progressive ticket with LaFollette, as a protest against Republican corruption and Democratic control by Wall Street. Thus the progressives of both parties were joined. Wheeler made a strenuous campaign in which one of his celebrated dramatic touches was to pull an empty chair to the front of the platform and then, with finger wagging and the New England nasal accents suggestive of Cal, to launch a series of questions, beginning with "Why did you sit silent when Fall was looting the country's oil reserves, Mr. Cullidge?" After each question he waited for an answer from "Silent Cal," sometimes putting his hand behind his ear, while the audience shrieked with merriment.

As a matter of fact, Wheeler loves to be the "bad boy" a little too much for his own good, but when he controls his instinct for being "contrary" it is devastating. For example, in 1930 he was invited to speak at the National Democratic Club in New York by Jouett Shouse, then John Raskob's handyman. Wheeler went and said that the next Democratic nominee ought to be a liberal and that he ought to be Roosevelt. The Raskob-Shouse combination, which even then was strongly anti-Roosevelt and determined to force the nomination of a conservative Wall Street Democrat, was thrown into consternation by this typical Wheeler performance.

III

It was Wheeler's astuteness and consistency in supporting the Roosevelt candidacy from an early date which makes his present loyalty to the New Deal so important an element in Roosevelt's calculations. Burt was the first prominent Democrat outside the State of New York to declare for Roosevelt for President and this was before Roosevelt's triumphant reëlection as Governor had established F.D.R.'s reputation as a phenomenal vote-getter with the ability to break down Republican party lines. Wheeler was one of the first to begin active pre-convention work for Roosevelt, being a powerful factor in lining up the Western and Mountain delegations for F.D.R. and in convincing George Norris, and later Bob LaFollette, that Roosevelt was the white hope of American liberals. Wheeler was one of the Roosevelt "inner circle" at Chicago and was unquestionably disappointed when he failed to receive the Vice-Presidential nomination. Later on he became sulky, as Roosevelt talked up "sound money" and was cautious in the silver policy.

What made Wheeler really angry with the New Deal, however, was the fact that when Roosevelt finally decided to "do something" for silver, he chose Key Pittman of Nevada rather than Wheeler, the traditional Free Silverite, as his agent. Wheeler claimed and still claims that Pittman is a "faker on silver," that, while Pittman also wants to "do something" for silver, he is not a thorough-going "16 to 1" Free Silverite according to the gospel of William Jennings Bryan. (Which is probably the reason Roosevelt used Pittman instead of Wheeler.)

Being a crank on money and a subscriber to the theory that all economic problems of the farmer can be solved by monetary inflation, without changing any other elements in the picture, Wheeler was suspicious of the A.A.A. As an old-fashioned trust-buster, he was highly critical of N.R.A. Wheeler really devoutly believes in bimetallism as the answer to the woes of the capitalistic world and is still living back in 1896, in his economic thought. Another of his pet schemes—the nationalization of the railroads—was also lifted from Bryan and, as an ambitious politician, he will take on any other issues that look as though they might lead to something.

The truth is that Wheeler is rather lazy mentally. He hasn't kept up with the industrial procession and hasn't analyzed the implications of central banking credit in relation to specie, of technology in relation to production, and of ownership in relation to distribution. His early success in 1924, at the age of forty, lulled him into a mood of unwarranted self-confidence. If he would study current problems as Bob Wagner and young Bob LaFollette study them, he would be a much more effective man.

The truth is that Wheeler is at bottom a gambler as well as a fighter. He has always taken political long shots. He loves the excitement of politics as some men love the tension of the Stock Exchange and is an independent "operator," who tries to show that he can do what cooler politicians say can't be done. The "16 to 1" theme of Free Silver is at his very core. He will run when there is only one chance out of sixteen of winning and after all

no man from Montana—with its minute electoral vote—
can expect to reach the Presidency except as a long-shot
gambler.

For this reason, he is being watched closely. If the time
looks propitious in 1936, he may suddenly come to the
fore, with the support of Huey Long, the Farmer-
Laborites, some of the Progressives (though not the La-
Follettes), and with the hope of aid from Coughlin. If
things don't work out right for his plans, he may support
someone else, in the hope of getting the nomination as a
liberal Democrat or as a Third Party leader for himself in
1940. Thus he might logically become the man to re-
unite the dissatisfied left wingers to a more liberal Democratic Party in 1940.

Wheeler has been feeling out the other Progressives
about forming a legislative alliance of liberal Democrats
and progressive Republicans—the old problem of making
prima donnas sing in chorus which has baffled the liberals
for years. He is not ready to break openly with Roosevelt,
for whose political skill he has great admiration and much
of whose program he favors. However, he has nothing to
worry about personally, with a firm grip on his own State
—he was reëlected in 1928, year of the Hoover landslide
and again in 1934, by a phenomenal majority—and he can
skip in and out of the party at his own sweet will, as he
did in 1924, without fear of political punishment.

There is one further factor in his political strength
which is difficult to classify—the fact that he is the father
of six children. The human race still sub-consciously
worships fertility and responds instinctively to men of
large families—like Roosevelt and Al Smith. His family
life is pleasant and modest. They live very quietly in
Washington during the winters and spend much of the
long nonpolitical summers camping in Glacier National

Park. One of Wheeler's daughters, Elizabeth, has already emerged as a radical youth leader and one of his sons works for Floyd Olson. Is another political dynasty akin to the Roosevelts in New York and the LaFollettes in Wisconsin forming in the Northwest?

Wheeler, tall, rangy, intelligent and vigorous as most transplanted New Englanders, will bear watching. He is a good gamble for those who like to play long shots but he is too erratic for those who operate on safe political margins.

VIII

NEEDLES IN THE HAYSTACK

THE MIDDLE AND WESTERN STATES are crawling with radical farm leaders whose individual influence may be small and localized but whose aggregate power to make or break Administrations would be great, if they are ever brought together in a national campaign. Such a leader is A. C. Townley, chief organizer of the Non-Partisan League back in 1915, who dropped out of sight for several years only to reappear as independent candidate for Governor of Minnesota in 1934, when, incidentally, he made a poor showing against Olson. Such a man is "Alfalfa Bill" Murray of Oklahoma, who was a name to conjure with two or three years ago but who has since been repealed. There are dozens of such minor leaders in all the agrarian States —Farmers' Union men, heads of the more radical locals of other organizations, men who spring up swiftly in the wake of a leader who is strong enough to set the pace.

In "good times," when farm prices are high and rains are plentiful, there is little but besotted conservatism in this region, but come two or three seasons of low prices and short crops and the West awakens and demands political action to redress this manifest injustice. Such have been the circumstances of the last few years—drought, grasshoppers, loss of markets abroad and of urban purchasing power in the United States—that many wheat and corn-and-hog farmers of the American steppes have been rendered desperate, despite the munificence of the A.A.A. There are now more needles than hay in the national hay-

stack and politicians groping for votes in the dark and
bloody ground west of the water-tower are likely to prick
their fingers.

In the case of the New Deal calculus, certain problems
which haunted the early days of the Roosevelt Administration have been canceled out. The old-time Western
Progressives—the men who followed T.R. to Armageddon
in 1912—are not likely to desert F.D.R. for the black eyes
of Huey Long in 1936. For example, neither Hiram Johnson of California nor George Norris of Nebraska is likely
to abandon the New Deal in 1936, unless it goes completely over to the right wing, as Wilson's New Freedom
did twenty years ago. Both have got so much that they
want out of the New Deal and have fought so many losing
battles in the past, that they are not likely to risk what
they have won by promoting a Third Party, the most
logical result of which would be the election of a Republican conservative in the ensuing campaign. Similarly, Senator James Couzens of Michigan—"the Scab Millionaire,"
as Ray Tucker aptly labeled him—has been supporting the
New Deal as a whole, although he did not support Roosevelt in 1932, and is not the type of man to go whoring
after strange candidates in 1936.

The Middle Western core of progressive and liberal
sentiment is still thoroughly committed to the Roosevelt
experiment and the dangers to his continued grip on the
Northern Mississippi Valley must be sought on the rim
of the farm belt rather than at its center, in the Bad Lands
(politically as well as agriculturally) rather than on the
rich black soil of the central prairies.

II

Ned Costigan, Democratic Senator from the State of
Colorado, will stay hitched to the New Deal bandwagon

so long as Roosevelt stays hitched to recognizably liberal principles, but will never follow any man against his own convictions.

Edward P. Costigan could never be a demagogue. He is a quiet-spoken man, with a resonant and beautiful voice, punctiliously polite in all of his political and social contacts, whose short slender body, deep black eyes, and parchment-like face, render him a fascinating as well as a forceful figure. He talks like a social welfare worker or a school teacher but packs a big progressive punch as innocently as a returning traveler packs an extra quart of Scotch. He is fearless, independent, and has in addition to a first-class mind, a fine background of scholarship. His sincerity rings as true as that of George Norris and his eyes reveal an unflagging intensity of purpose.

He was born sixty-one years ago of a substantial Virginia family. When Ned was a boy, his father went West and bought a silver mine, which he resold before he knew it would yield a fortune. Costigan went to Harvard, where he specialized in economics, political science and history. Compelled by illness to drop out, he traveled abroad, studied law and was admitted to the Utah bar before he returned to Harvard to complete his academic course and get his degree in 1899, the year before F.D.R. entered Harvard.

Costigan returned to Colorado—which shares the distinction with West Virginia of being the arch "kept" State of the Union—to find that this principality of high finance lacked all of the essential elements of the democracy which he had come to admire in his studies. When he ran for the State Legislature as an independent the Republicans refused to seat him because he would not pledge himself to vote for their candidate for the U. S. Senate. A Costigan never compromises his principles and he was

never given the seat to which his election entitled him.
This experience pitchforked him into reform politics in
Colorado. He helped organize an Honest Election League,
the Law Enforcement League, the Direct Primary League,
the Direct Legislation League and the "Dry Denver" campaign. He was also organizer of the Citizens Party, which
won the municipal election in Denver in 1912, and in the
same year, he organized the Progressive Party in Colorado
and was its candidate for Governor in 1912 and again
two years later.

1914 was the year of the great Colorado coal strike,
which led to a Congressional investigation and a modification of the Rockefeller labor policies. Costigan had just
been nominated for the Governorship when the United
Mine Workers called on him to defend some of their
members who had been indicted for murder. He knew
that if he took the case he had no chance to be elected
Governor, for in bloody industrial warfare of this type
the middle and farming classes tend to go conservative. He
took the case, lost the election, and carried the accused
miners' defense through a laborious series of trials for
two years, finally winning acquittals for all of them in
1916. He also represented the miners during the Congressional investigations of the Colorado "war."

It was in this long fight that he became such a close
friend of Josephine Roche (now named, at his instance, to
the post of Assistant Secretary of the Treasury), who soon
afterward showed Colorado what enlightened management could do. Costigan became General Counsel for her
Rocky Mountain Fuel Company, which gave the hostile
mining czars of Colorado a demonstration of the feasibil-
ity of coöperation with organized labor. In 1916, following
Theodore Roosevelt's abandonment of the Progressive
cause, Costigan threw his support to Wilson whom he con-

sidered more liberal than Hughes. The next year, Wilson paid his debt by appointing Costigan to the Tariff Commission, where he remained until he resigned in 1928. He accompanied his resignation with a powerful attack on Coolidge's manipulation and packing of the Commission, and returned to enter Colorado politics.

In 1930 he sought the Democratic nomination for the Senate, beat the machine in the primary and won the election, although he had voted to lower the duty on sugar, while a member of the Tariff Commission, and Colorado is the great beet-sugar producing State of the West. In 1932, Costigan again helped beat the reactionary Democratic machine, backing Alva Adams for Senator. Adams was nominated and elected but, in the manner of many liberals, immediately went conservative and in 1934 lined up with the Democratic old guard to defeat Costigan's candidate for the Democratic nomination for Governor of Colorado: Josephine Roche.

In the Senate, Costigan has been an alert and zealous Progressive, who seldom gets out in front and is rarely sensational. When the time arrives for a penetrating, carefully worded question to demolish the opposition, Costigan is there. It is a pity that he did not conduct the banking investigation of 1933 for his own occasional questions were far more effective than Pecora's rain-on-a-tin-roof style of cross-examination. Costigan, a tried crusader, was prepared to join a Third Party movement in 1932 if Roosevelt had failed to secure the Democratic nomination, and will stick to Roosevelt so long as Roosevelt remains progressive. If the New Deal goes over to the Tories, as a result of either conservative boring from within or political expediency, Ned Costigan will be found out on the progressive battle line, for he is a man who feels deeply, thinks clearly, speaks with restraint, acts vigorously, and does not compromise. On this account, he should be watched, for as Costigan goes so goes the vote of thousands of liberals throughout the West.

III

Other leaders who will be found in the progressive camp when the tocsin sounds, are Homer T. Bone and Lewis Baxter Schwellenbach, Senior and Junior Senator, respectively, from the State of Washington. Like Senator Bone, Schwellenbach is an incessant liberal, though his career has been less stormy than that of Bone, who has run as a Progressive, a Socialist, a Republican and a Democrat.

Bone, the senior of the Washington duet of liberals, had run for office on the Republican, Progressive, and Socialist tickets, before he came to the Senate as a Democrat in the 1932 election. He is a native Hoosier, aged 52, who has spent his adult life in the Northwest and he is a lawyer by profession. But he has lavished most of his legal talents on the financially unprofitable business of defending underdogs. In politics his greatest interest has been public ownership of power, and he was one of the chief organizers of the movement toward public ownership. He put through the Bone bill authorizing cities owning power plants of their own to sell excess power anywhere in the state of Washington. This law was upheld by popular referendum.

Bone also has been a consistent pal of the A. F. of L.— but this ancient body is pretty radical in Washington. The only "vested interests" with which he has kept on really good terms are the timber and pulpwood companies. Like so many of the Western liberals he is a hardy nationalist who voted against the World Court, and he is not above making capital of the "Yellow Peril." He boasts of a grandfather who fought in the Union Army in the Civil War and since coming to Washington has made a hobby of retracing his illustrious ancestor's movements on the battlefields near Washington. A forceful orator, he indulges in no little flag-waving. Perhaps it is good protective coloration for his militant liberalism—a type which would be called "Communist" in the loose and ready lingo of Wall Street.

On the floor of the Senate, Bone has been quiet. But he is a conscientious worker in committees and exceptionally clever in detecting jokers in bills—especially where his old friend, Power, is concerned. He has been one of the most painstaking workers on the Nye munitions investigating committee. He has supported the New Deal on most test votes, and his occasional strayings have been to the liberal or pro-labor side.

Bone is one of the few men in the Senate who appreciates the significance of the great Columbia River power and irrigation developments—which are so frequently derided as "white elephants." Bone sees that if they are carried to completion they will open hundreds of thousands of acres of new land and will permit a great industrial development in the Northwest based on water transportation and oceans of cheap electricity. This will afford new outlets for hundreds of thousands of persons driven from the submarginal and dust-storm areas of the western plains. Bone is building his future, as he has built his political past, very largely on electric power.

Old-fashioned Tories would regard Schwellenbach also as a "Communist." Actually he is nothing but a progressive of the same stripe as Bone and Wheeler and is a fair representative of the State in which the unemployed have organized themselves as a political faction and have demanded real work relief instead of the dole. Schwellenbach was born in Wisconsin in 1894, the youngest of four children (curious how the Wisconsin tradition has spread!), but was only eight years old when his father died and the family moved to Spokane, Washington. There "Lewie" sold newspapers, attended high school, and studied history and public speaking under one Clarence C. Dill, whom Schwellenbach later succeeded in the Senate. In 1914, the family moved on to Seattle and Lewis entered the University of Washington, where he was a classmate of Emil Hurja, now Jim Farley's demon statistician and executive assistant. Schwellenbach got a law degree and set up practice in Seattle, where he did reasonably well, serving at various times as director of a bank, a brewery and a laundry.

He has a deep, slow voice, which speeds up in the heat of a political oration, and his law practice frequently brought him into the position of representing labor unions and farm organizations in the courts. At an early age he became interested in the power question and in 1928, at the age of twenty-eight, he presided at the first Washington State Power Conference. His successor as chairman of this conference was Homer T. Bone. Government ownership of power projects has been one of Schwellenbach's main planks for years, which accounts largely for the conservative hatred of his "Communism"—it being obvious to certain minds that it is morally wrong for the Government to own or operate anything which could be turned into a profitable enterprise under private ownership.

In 1932, Schwellenbach sought public office for the first time. He wanted to be Governor but was beaten in the Democratic primary by Clarence D. Martin. Martin was elected in the November elections and appointed Schwellenbach a member of the Board of Regents of the University of Washington. This same year, Schwellenbach proposed to meet the unemployment problem by putting the unemployed to work in idle factories and on idle lands. It was an "End Poverty in Washington" program, although not advanced under that name, and Schwellenbach claims that Sinclair got EPIC from him. In 1934, when Dill decided to retire from the Senate, Schwellenbach sought the nomination, winning a hot primary campaign and being overwhelmingly elected in November. During the primary and general campaigns he still argued for his unemployment plan, which became known as EPIW. As the campaign wore on, Schwellenbach toned down his "radicalism" somewhat and campaigned on a "support the President" platform, with special emphasis on old age and unemployment insurance, cheaper electricity, and—by way of "left deviation from the party line"—payment of the bonus. He comes by his bonus policy honestly, for he was in the army during the war, had been State Commander of the Legion in Washington, and has favored the bonus for years.

He has not yet had time to make much of an impression in the Senate, as he is new and hasn't tried to advertise himself by dramatic tactics. With Bone, however, he stands as proof that the Northwest corner of the United States is thoroughly progressive and that its attachment to Roosevelt may endure only so long as the latter can convince the State of Washington that he is an unflinching liberal. On the other hand, there remains the possibility that a "vigilante" type of campaign, such as that which defeated Sinclair in California, if given Administration countenance, might shake the progressive Democratic grip on the State. The effect of this, in a three-cornered fight, would be to throw Washington back into the control of the Seattle gang and the Chamber of Commerce Republicans. Liberalism in politics on the West Coast—as at Washington—has yet to prove its staying power.

IV

There is less doubt about the durability of the Dakota progressives. The area which produced such figures as Townley, Langer, Frazier and Nye, can be depended upon to put up a fight for its principles and to fight even when it hasn't any.

One of these men, Gerald Nye, now Junior Senator from North Dakota, is in many ways the most intriguing and attractive figure. Nye has made himself a national figure at the age of forty-two, either because the average newspaperman is especially well-equipped to make a first-rate legislator, because the U. S. Senate is singularly lacking in talents, or because of pure luck—or because of all three factors in combination. Not that Nye lacks ability; he has plenty of it, but in ten years in the Senate he has shown repeatedly not only that newspaper training may show one how to get in the limelight but that it is superior to the average legal training for the conduct of a Senatorial investigation.

Like Schwellenbach, Nye is a native of Wisconsin. He was born in Hortonsville, Wisconsin, where his father edited a village paper and was a strong LaFollette supporter. Young Nye went to high school at Wittenburg, Wisconsin, and returned at the age of nineteen to begin newspaper work in Hortonsville. He worked for and edited several small town papers in Wisconsin and Iowa and moved to North Dakota only when the war made it a boom area, as the prairie was plowed up for wheat and wheat prices mounted. Nye bought a small paper and for a time it was the only privately-owned journal which supported the rising Non-Partisan League. In 1919, he became editor and manager of the Griggs County "Sentinel-Courier," which had been purchased by a group of Non-Partisan farmers. This was his true introduction to a political career.

The Non-Partisan League won control of the State and set it to building grain-elevators and flour-mills, in an effort to beat down the "interests." Our most advanced experiment in State socialism was under way. Lynn J. Frazier, now U. S. Senator, was Governor, and Nye backed the League. The League had its ups and downs, tending to decline with the price of wheat, but in 1925 one of its two representatives in the Senate, Dr. Edwin F. Ladd, who had taught chemistry in the State Agricultural College, died. The McNary-Haugen movement was then going at full blast and Nye was one of a group who brought pressure to have Ladd's seat filled at once, so that the full strength favoring the McNary-Haugen measure would be represented in the coming session of Congress.

Governor Sorlie, a Non-Partisan Leaguer, held off and there were some legal difficulties and some suspicion that Sorlie was trying to hold off to the end of his term as Governor so that he could take the Senatorship himself. Finally Sorlie gave in and appointed Nye, who was not a candidate and had never held any office higher than a local school trustee. Nye thought at first that it was a practical joke, but then packed up and came to Washington in December, 1925. The regular Republicans were in full control of the Senate and they made the most of the legal question of Sorlie's right to fill the Senate vacancy by appointment. Finally, when his funds were almost exhausted, Nye convinced a bare majority that he was entitled to his seat. A few months later he ran for the balance of the term, as an independent against a conservative Republican, and won. In the fall of 1926 he was again elected, this time for the full term of six years.

The 1926 election knocked out a number of conservative Republicans and put prairie politicians at a premium. The general shift of chairmanships resulted in Nye's reaching the chairmanship of the important Public Lands Committee, sixteen months after his arrival in Washington. As such, he presided over the second oil scandal investigation, which revealed how Harry F. Sinclair helped to repay the Republican National Committee for the lease of Teapot Dome. Walsh of Montana was the prosecutor but Nye got in some shrewd strokes of his own, including the revelation that Andrew Mellon, the impeccable Secretary of the Treasury, had been asked by Will Hays to take some of the Sinclair Liberty Bonds and had come across with a $50,000 contribution instead and, although he had the key to the knowledge that the Senate Committee had been seeking for ten months, had kept quiet about it. Andy Mellon was never more uncomfortable than when Nye inquired:

"This committee has been trying for two months to trace these bonds, and its failure up to the last few days has been front page news in all the newspapers. Will you tell us why you did not give us the information you had before this?"

It was Nye who, as Chairman of the Senatorial Campaign Investigating Committee, uncovered Bob Lucas' "Grocer Norris" plot in Nebraska, and finally disclosed how Bishop Cannon had used unreported campaign contributions against Al Smith in 1928. His biggest break came in the munitions investigation. The idea was handed to him by some women pacifists who were convinced that the commercial interest in munition-mongering was a fruitful cause of international conflict and Nye, as a good newspaper man, saw its potentialities at once. The munitions investigation, with its extraordinary revelation of the social and moral implications of permitting the manufacture of big-time lethal devices to be conducted for private profit, has made Nye a national figure.

Nye confined his 1932 activities to ensuring his own reelection and did not support Hoover. He teamed up with Bill Borah in 1934, in leading the attack on the N.R.A. but joined with the Democrats to elect a Democratic Governor of North Dakota the same year, because Nye distrusted Langer who, after being convicted, tried to do a Jim Ferguson act by running his wife for the Governorship. Nye's own political ambitions seem to lie in the Republican Party for the present. As a political descendant of the "free-soilers" who got the land of the prairies as a gift from the Party of Lincoln, he sees a chance to make the Party of Ogden Mills progressive once again and has been booming former Governor Winant of New Hampshire for the Presidential nomination, the tacit assumption being that Nye would be the Vice-Presidential candidate on the same ticket. If the Republicans are convinced they are going to lose anyhow in 1936, the conservatives might give Nye the Vice-Presidential nomination, just to keep him and his kind happy, with the hope that they will stay in line for a real Republican push in 1940.

If, however, a vigorous progressive movement materialized on national lines, Nye would be hard to hold. Huey Long might force his hand, for the Kingfish could make a strong appeal to the North Dakota wild men—and the State is wilder than ever as a result of the depression, the drought and the general cussedness of human nature in a time of confusion.

V

Symptomatic of the State's perennial attitude of having tarantulas in its political pants is the shifting frenzy which sent Bill Langer to the Governor's chair, saw him found guilty of conspiracy to defraud the United States in the operation of Federal relief funds, and hurled him from power to scheme his political revenge.

Unlike Nye, William Langer was actually born in North Dakota. He saw the light of day forty-nine years ago on a farm, the grandson of one of the first settlers of the State, graduated from the University of North Dakota with a law degree, and began the practice of law. Soon afterward he came East to Columbia University, where he was the valedictorian of the class of 1910, and married a New York girl, Lydia Cady, the daughter of that John Cleveland Cady who designed the Metropolitan Opera House and other well-known buildings of the period.

Langer brought his wife back to North Dakota, where he practiced law in earnest in the town of Mandan, built up a good legal business and was elected first county prosecutor and then State Attorney-General for the 1916–1920 stretch. He followed this by settling down to a big law practice in Bismarck, where he also became a bank director. In 1920 he won the Republican nomination for the Governorship but was licked by Lynn J. Frazier, then running for the third time on a Non-Partisan League ticket. In 1932, Langer was nominated and elected, the Republican Party having absorbed most of the Non-Partisan League in the meantime, but he was soon on the outs with most of the League leaders, including Nye and Frazier. Langer was no conservative. He lambasted the New Deal, put embargoes on cattle and wheat shipments and almost matched the record of "Alfalfa Bill" Murray in calling out the National Guard. He even came East and, standing on the steps of the White House, let a blast against the New Deal for the benefit of newspaper men.

In March, 1934, Harry Hopkins removed him as head of the State relief agency, charging that he was making F.E.R.A. employees contribute to his political newspaper, "The Leader." Later Langer and four others were convicted of conspiracy to defraud the Government. (The cases are on appeal.) In the course of this trial, Langer explained the transfer of $19,000 from the accounts of "The Leader" to his own funds, by saying it was repayment to himself of money he had advanced for campaign expenses.

Langer fought to the last, calling out the National Guard to fend off removal, charging Nye with graft, trying to get the Legislature to investigate, and desperately seeking every means of escaping the inevitable. For a time it looked as if the Federal Government might be called upon to intervene. Then he gave up and his former ally, Lieutenant-Governor Ole H. Olson, moved into his chair. Langer had been renominated while under indictment but his conviction made him ineligible, so his wife was nominated. Nye, Frazier and their wing of the Non-Partisan League dropped the Langer team and backed Thomas Moodie, the Democratic candidate, and elected him. Now the opposition is trying to remove Moodie on the ground that he switched his residence to Minnesota and never reëstablished it in North Dakota.

The Langer influence is far from dead and if it dies, someone will spring up to take his place, for North Dakota is the native haunt of political wild men and can be counted upon to join enthusiastically in any first-class economic scalping party.

VI

In view of the heated character of prairie politics it is probable that the best way to promote a political cause west of the Mississippi is to avoid public office, with its impeachments and its auditors. Milo Reno, the Iowa firebrand, who has combined a profitable insurance business with a radical farm program for many years, is too wise to jeopardize his influence by accepting legal responsibility of any sort.

Reno is the man who gave the nation the Farm Holiday movement, the "penny auctions" against mortgage foreclosures, and the "milk strikes." These weapons of desperate farmers, first tried in Iowa, became a national institution in 1932 and 1933 and did much to put a real head of steam back of the opening phases of the New Deal. With the success of the Roosevelt Administration in relieving some of the pressure of farm debt and boosting the price of basic farm commodities, Reno and his following began to slip.

Milo Reno was born in Agency, Iowa. He is seventy years old. He comes by his "radicalism" legitimately. His father was a fireman and a Granger and his mother was a Greenbacker and later a Populist. Milo went to Oklaloosa College in Iowa and studied theology but has been a bona fide farmer and for many years he has been active in the Farmers' Union. In 1920 he was a rather obscure delegate to an Iowa State convention of the Farmers' Union and attracted attention by his speeches which were and still are of the school of William Jennings Bryan.

He is now President of the National Farm Holiday Association. He runs some mutual insurance companies which carry life, automobile, and fire insurance, and in 1932 he admitted that his average annual income for the past twelve years has been $8,000. He now lives in Des Moines, and rides one of his thoroughbred horses every morning. He has thick, curly black hair streaked with gray and deep-set eyes. His personality is friendly and likeable.

For many years he was State President of the Farmers' Union in Iowa, which has a fluctuating membership of between 10 and 12 thousand in Iowa. In most of Iowa, the counter organization, the Farm Bureau Federation, organized by the Chicago Board of Trade, is very strong —40,000 to 50,000 members in the State—the largest farm organization in the United States.

He plays ball with the LaFollettes and Olson and recently predicted that Floyd Olson would be the next President of the United States. He is down on Washington, where he has been pretty generally snubbed. Reno himself does not have personal political ambitions—he's too old—but he does play adroit politics, bargaining with Iowa candidates. The coöperatives which the Farmers' Union started in Iowa have not been successful.

He was instrumental in starting the Farm Holiday movement, but it got beyond his control. The I.W.W.'s have left a deep radical impression in the cornfields of Iowa and once the farmers started "direct action" tactics, they wouldn't stop where Reno wanted them to stop. During the strike, Mary Ellen Vease's old slogan, "Raise less corn and more hell," became increasingly popular.

Reno always denies any tinge of radicalism. He says, "They call us radicals. We're not. All we ask is that the farmers who produce the nation's food shall receive in return the cost of production."

He realized that the strike was more effective as propaganda to keep the farmers' troubles on page one than it was as an economic weapon. He advocates currency inflation, refinancing of farm mortgages at low interest rates, and coöperation between the farmer and the laborer:

"I'll tell you who will suffer when the farmer and the workingman get together, as they are going to do. It's the usurer. It's the middleman who preys upon both, without performing any useful service. He's got to have his claws clipped," says Reno.

His first practical gesture for Third Party politics was made in 1934 when he came to New York and suggested a plan to LaGuardia that idle factories, rolling stock of railroads, etc., be placed at the disposal of unemployed workmen and that they exchange goods for farm products.

He still has a tireless denunciatory rhetoric, plenty of energy, despite his 70 years, and an urge to power. He is a shrewd business man and a big, rather attractive Mid-Western farmer-politician who let himself be whipsawed out of control of the farmers of his section by Rooseveltian charm and Henry Wallace's timely allotment checks. Since 1933 Reno has lost control of the Farmers' Union in Iowa, but he has not let up with his agitating. Although his main influence is still centered in Iowa and South Dakota, his "milk strike" program left him with strong allies among the continuously bitched dairy farmers of the Northeastern States. He can usually turn out from five to ten thousand farmers of the less prosperous type— mostly tenants—for a rally or parade, but is too intent on making farming a capitalistic business in which a profit is guaranteed to cultivate durable relations with the urban radicals.

For months rumors have gone around that the Republicans are subsidizing him, and Theodore Roosevelt, Jr. is supposed to have visited him a few weeks back. At the end of April, 1935, he held a mass meeting of New Deal dissenters at Des Moines to which he invited Long, Coughlin, Olson, Townsend, and others, but only Long appeared on the scene.

Reno has been a bitter critic of Henry Wallace, of Roosevelt and the A.A.A. He supports the Farmers' Union program: cost of production guaranteed to the farmer, reduction of interest on farm mortgages to one per cent or less. All Western agrarian programs are about identical and the significance of Reno is not his program but the fact that he taught the Western farmers how to use direct action in 1932–33. The marching farm armies in State Capitols—they are still marching in the drought areas—were the result of his leadership. Under his banner in Iowa, all kinds of Reds have enlisted to take a try at direct action, and in 1933 he even drew a certain number of Communist sympathizers from the East.

He is temporarily at a disadvantage because Iowa is doing relatively well out of the New Deal, but he is the key to the poorer-class farmer and the less prosperous tenants in this, the richest farming section of the country, and he has kept clear enough of conventional politics to provide a good neutral rallying-ground for the left wingers.

The difficulty with his program, as indeed with the program of most Western agrarian leaders, is the fact that American farming is *not* a business but that the farmer *is* a business man. Much unctuous sentiment is breathed about the fact that farming is "a way of life," whatever that means, as well as about the natural wonders of country life and the nobility of the farmer. The truth is, of course, that farming is largely a residue of those economic activities which have not been industrially specialized and hence is bound to become progressively less economic and less profitable as specialization catches up with agriculture. This is the rock which has shattered every political

effort to find a satisfactory place for individual farm
properties in an industrial capitalistic system.

The second, and equally great difficulty is the fact that
the American farmer on the average, being a petty capitalist, though playing a losing game, is property-minded to
an almost incredible degree. His interest is not in the co-
operative commonwealth, in industrial democracy, a balanced economy, or economic or social justice. His interest
is in getting the largest possible personal income from
his farm, with the least conceivable amount of outside
interference. Hence the bright and hopeful efforts to team
him up with the urban radicals in any movement more
far-reaching than the Scandinavian type of coöperation
proposed in Olson's Minnesota are doomed to crushing
disappointment, unless it is clearly understood that socialism is not to be applied to farming. Even those farmers at the bottom of the ladder, the white tenants and day-
labor and harvest-hands of the wheat and corn States, are
horrified at the idea of huge industrial farms, whether
privately controlled or operated on the order of the Russian collective farms, and are disposed to demand a chain-
store technique of graduated taxation to prevent scientific
farm production from displacing the traditional medium-
sized pioneer homestead.

For the farm belters are bourgeois to a man, and the
Mississippi Valley is inhabited by people whom Stalin
would term *kulaks* and Mussolini and Hitler would regard as peasants, and who offer little foothold for the
preaching of "scientific socialism." Hence a Third Party
movement which aspired to link them to the EPIC Plan-
ners of the West Coast and the industrial "proletarians"
and under-privileged groups of the East would have to
devise a formula by which the farmer would be left free

in an industrially socialized State. It is, in fact, only where the inherent disadvantages of trying to run farming on business lines have completed the agrarian cycle by divorcing agriculture from ownership, as in the sharecropper sections of the cotton belt, that "scientific socialism" has a chance. But between the economic radicals and the wheat and corn farmers of the West the latter's concept of private property still lies like a naked sword in the political marriage bed—it can be surmounted, but only at the risk of bloodshed.

IX

MARX ON THE HALF-SHELL

THE SOCIALIST PARTY faces two great obstacles in its effort to convert the American people to the Marxian theory. The first of these obstacles is the American people; the second is the Socialist Party.

Americans seem to have an invincible distaste for anything complex, articulate or precise in the way of political theory. They will fight to "free the slaves" or "make the world safe for democracy" but won't bother to register their votes for or against industrial democracy or the co-operative commonwealth. The Marxians, on the other hand, whether of Socialist or Communist persuasion, have made political theory a subject only slightly less complicated than a fifty-move queen's pawn's defense set-to between Lasker and Capablanca. Worse still, from the American point of view, is the fact that the Socialist Party is confined largely to foreign-language circles in a few major cities—New York, Milwaukee, Chicago—and is alien in blood as well as in doctrine.

Except for the truly contemptible leadership of American Communism and its subservience to the political interests of the government of the Soviet Union, the party of "direct action" would long since have displaced the party of propaganda as head and front of the Marxian movement in the United States. As it is, American Communism is still a negligible force which confines itself to trouble-making and religious squabbles as to Party doctrine, while American Socialism, with the help of highly literate white-collar propagandists such as Norman Thomas, has become the most powerful educative force in American politics.

In fact, the historic mission of American Socialism seems to be to anticipate and formulate the policies which the major parties must adopt. Hence it has the unique, if somewhat gloomy prospect of being always a bridesmaid but never a bride in the matter of national policy. It is dead right about the fact that a marriage is taking place but it is never found in the double-bed of practical politics on election night.

A glance at some of the principal planks of the Socialist Party Program for the Presidential election of 1932 reveals the interesting fact that the main outlines of the "New Deal," which partisan critics of the Roosevelt Administration are unable to locate in the Democratic Party program of that year, were quite definitely indicated by Mr. Norman Thomas and his half-shell Marxists:

1. Entry of the United States into the League of Nations. (Checked by the Senate defeat of the World Court Protocol)

2. Federal appropriation of five billion dollars for immediate relief and an additional five billions for a public works program. (Cf. P.W.A., F.E.R.A. and the current Work Relief measure)

3. Six-hour day and five-day week without reduction in pay. (Approached through the Connery Bill)

4. A minimum wage. (N.R.A.)

5. Government unemployment insurance. (Current Social Security Program)

6. Old age pensions. (Ditto)

7. Health and maternity insurance. (Ditto)

8. Improved workmen's compensation and accident insurance. (State laws)

9. Abolition of child labor. (N.R.A.)

10. Laws facilitating the organization of labor unions and prohibiting "yellow dog" contracts. (N.R.A.)

11. Steeply increased inheritance taxes and income taxes of the higher incomes. (Revenue Act of 1934—but not high enough to please the Socialists)

12. Tax on all government securities. (Under consideration but constitutional amendment is probably necessary)

13. A two-year moratorium on foreclosures and tax sales of farms and homes, with suspension of all interest payments, for this period. (Farm Credit Administration, H.O.L.C. and State laws)

14. Socialization of power, banking and other industries. (Approached in T.V.A. yardstick, proposed Amendments to Federal Reserve Act, Deposit Insurance, etc.)

15. Lowering of farm taxes. (Recommended to State and County governments)

16. Establishment of Federal marketing agencies and extension of agricultural coöperatives. (Approached through A.A.A. marketing agreements)

17. Economic, political and legal equality for negroes. (Not while the South is in the Saddle)

18. Drastic anti-lynching laws. (Ditto, but consider the Costigan-Wagner Bill)

19. Disarmament, not as a panacea but to make a sudden war less likely. (State Department policy but abandoned as a unilateral attitude as result of European and Far Eastern situation)

20. Cancellation of war debts and reparations, provided such action is linked with disarmament. (Done without our open consent)

21. The end of collecting private debts in weak nations by military force and of such "imperialism" as America

has practiced in Haiti and Nicaragua. (Done by Executive action)

22. Agreement with other nations not to finance or furnish war supplies to an aggressor nation which ignores its treaty obligations. (Proposed by current Administration draft of neutrality laws and by proposed embargoes)

23. Tariff reductions. (The Reciprocal Trade Agreements Act of 1934)

24. A world conference on a fiscal system and allocation of raw materials. (The London Economic Conference of 1933)

25. Philippine independence. (Done by Act of Congress—but it takes ten years)

26. Public employment exchanges. (Done by Wagner Bills of 1932–33)

To this comprehensive program, Mr. Thomas added the observation in his campaign pamphlet, "The Socialist Cure for a Sick Society," that "These things will not take place or will be relatively futile until we press actual change in ownership of land, natural resources and principal means of production." (See the Land Policy Section of the Department of Agriculture, the Power Commission, Utilities Holding Company proposals, the T.V.A., and the program of the National Resources Board.)

The leader of this Socialist campaign of education, Norman Mattoon Thomas, was born in Marion, Ohio, fifty-one years ago, the son of a Presbyterian minister, and was conventional enough to decide at an early age that the eldest son should follow his father's profession. As a boy, Thomas made only one conventional "political" gesture; he carried newspapers for none other than that eminent small-town newspaper, "The Marion Star," owned by the late Warren Gamaliel Harding.

As a minister's son, young Thomas was born into an

energetically fermenting "social consciousness." His
mother took an active interest in community affairs and
when the family moved to Lewisbury, Pennsylvania, she
became a member of the local school board. Book learning is also traditionally valued in a clergyman's home and
Norman was frequently found with his nose in a book
although the cult of "muscular Christianity" induced him
to select as his favorite exercise boxing, in which he became a neighborhood champion.

After a listless freshman year at Bucknell, relatives enabled him to realize his ambition to attend Princeton,
where he earned part of his expenses and was distin-
guished for his scholarship and for his skill in debating.
He fell most strongly under the influence of Woodrow
Wilson, who was then teaching at "Old Nassau" and has
tended ever since to ape Wilson's rather pedantic style
of writing. There is also a great similarity in the rhetoric of these two men, who did so much to direct the
political thought of the American nation during the last
generation.

After his graduation he spent a couple of years as a
social worker in a "settlement house" in the ghastly Spring
Street slums of New York City, where his book learning
was heavily edited by the "higher criticism" of hunger,
unemployment and general human misery. Troubled in
heart, he took a trip around the world and on his return
became assistant pastor to the Christ Church Settlement.
There he met Frances Violet Stewart, a serious-minded
social worker of the Frances Perkins stripe, who was beginning to organize one of the first American clinics for
the treatment of tuberculosis. They were married in 1910.

At this stage, Thomas was still following the role of
clergyman, in the belief that religion would provide the
solution to the social problems of the age. He became

assistant to Dr. Henry Van Dyke, at the fashionable Fifth Avenue Brick Church, and continued his studies at Union Theological Seminary. When it came time for him to be examined by the august New York Presbytery, his views were an unorthodox rebellion against all the musty cant of the standardized tenets. Startled members of the Presbytery questioned this attractive and very masculine young rebel for an entire afternoon, at the end of which they permitted him to be ordained. It was Norman Thomas's first appearance in public print, for the newspapers featured the ordination of this "heretic," but that was before the War, and it was still considered genteel for a young clergyman to take a warm interest in humanity. Experience no doubt would later tone down much of such assertiveness.

So he and his young wife went to the American Parish in one of the most down-at-heels sections of East Harlem in New York City, where they remained six years. Then he became completely disillusioned with the idea that the religious "settlement house" was something much more than the old patronizing system of giving cast-off clothing and an occasional basket of food to the "deserving (and respectful) poor."

In the meantime, the World War had opened up to Norman Thomas a real political career, although he did not at first realize it. He opposed war in principle, announced that he would not fight and that he would give no support from his pulpit to the ideal of organized international massacre. Morris Hillquit was then, as usual, running for the Mayoralty on the Socialist ticket, and Thomas wrote Hillquit pledging his support. His pacifism had frightened his few wealthy parishioners, but Socialism on top of it was too much for them: Thomas resigned.

Since then he has been through with the ministry, although he has never been able to shake off his pulpit manner and the Communists delight in portraying him as an effete, effeminate curate.

With a few friends, Thomas then founded "The New World," which was almost immediately rechristened "The World Tomorrow." It was a pale pink magazine, which recently was merged with another liberal religious magazine. With the usual astuteness of Government bureaucrats, the Department of Justice concluded that Thomas was a dangerous revolutionist. During the War, their agents shadowed him constantly, tapped his telephone wires, opened his mail, and sent reams of illiterate notes to Washington reporting his "subversive" activities. Postmaster Burleson regarded Thomas as a menace, "worse than Debs," and tried to suppress "The World Tomorrow." The Government couldn't touch him under the Selective Service Act, for he was just beyond the age limit for the first draft and had too many children (he is the father of six children, five of whom are living) to be included in the second. Thomas was especially critical of the treatment accorded to jailed conscientious objectors during the War, and did not modify his attitude, as did many of his Socialist colleagues, including Upton Sinclair. Instead, with Roger N. Baldwin, Thomas helped to found the National Civil Liberties Union, now the American Civil Liberties Union.

It is amusing to note that the least defensible feature of capitalism—unearned income—was the means by which Norman Thomas was able to keep going as a Socialist leader. Mrs. Thomas had inherited a small but regular income, so that he did not need to worry or work for the necessities of his large family, although, unlike that great and vertically endowed "Radical," Oswald Garrison Villard, Thomas lived—and lives—in a simplicity which accords with his Socialist beliefs.

During the year 1921–22, he was associate editor of Villard's "Nation." Then he threw his time and energies into building up the League for Industrial Democracy, the successor of the old Intercollegiate Socialist Party.

He took a very active part in the 1926–27 wool workers' strike in Passaic, when he went to Passaic nearly every day and cheered the strikers on, getting money for them and seeing that it was equitably distributed. When the Sheriff of Bergen County dictated, in the manner conventional to the local authorities of a "kept State," that no more public meetings might be held by the strikers, Thomas decided to test the decision. He rented a vacant lot, where he began to praise the traditional liberalism of Thomas Jefferson. Big strike-duty cops jerked him into a police car and hurried him to a night in a distant jail, so remote that his friends failed to find him before morning, as he was unable to post a $10,000 bond. He was then released and the ban on meetings was held illegal. In the future, the police did not interfere with the strikers' gatherings.

He has never taken any of his personal political campaigns seriously and regards them as educational tours. In 1928, although he covered the country pretty thoroughly, he polled only slightly more than a quarter of a million votes, the lowest Socialist national vote since 1900. This, however, may be partly due to the practice in many precincts of not counting the Socialist vote or of throwing Socialist votes into whichever column is most convenient to the local bosses. At the time several newspapers commented on the dignity of Thomas's 1928 campaign, in contrast with the cat-and-dog grotesqueries of the Hoover-

Smith wrangle. Thomas said, with his characteristic irony, "I appreciate the flowers, only I wish the funeral hadn't been so complete."

He is today the hero of the timid college student and of the stenographer who has tried to read Spengler but has been discouraged by that awful task. He is the white-collar Socialist leader, the college professor of the proletarians, with the fluent pedantry of the professional teacher and pulpiteer, the rigid logic of the Wilsonian school of Presbyterian politics, and the heavy ironic humor of one who is bookish rather than realistic in his approach to life.

II

It was, in fact, both accidental and rather embarrassing for him to discover, after more than a decade of political agitation, that he had identified himself with a hot political issue in his effort to improve the lot of the Southern share-croppers. He had thereby stumbled upon one of the really explosive—dangerously so—questions in our national life.

In the spring of 1934, Norman Thomas began to proclaim that the share-croppers of the South were the real orphans of the New Deal storm. The South had inherited from the Civil War and Reconstruction period a large and unsatisfactory substitute for slavery in the form of share-croppers and tenant farmers. In 1932, forced sales of farms for delinquent taxes, bankruptcies and foreclosures on mortgages increased from 19.5 to 41.5 per thousand, until today 42% of the farms in the United States are run by tenants, with the Southern States leading with an average of 58% of the farms worked by non-owners for the benefit of landlords. In a recent report, the Rosenwald Committee stated that the average level of living of the Southern share-cropper is far below that of the European peasant, pointing out that the application of the financial principles of industrial capitalism to an agrarian economy has produced a situation in which

The furnishing of the tenant with seed and tools and food and clothing at the traditional margin of from 20 to 30 per cent above cash prices has taken on a new aspect since it has become possible for landowners to secure their needed funds from the Farm Credit Administration. . . . As a result the government finds itself an involuntary, if not unsuspecting, partner in usury.

The Rosenwald report bears out the impressions made on Norman Thomas in his visit to the south in February, 1934, at which time he bluntly stated that the cotton reduction program had not helped the share-cropper. At the time, the Department of Agriculture took cognizance of the facts but justified its own hand-washing policy by pointing out that the Agricultural Adjustment Act had given them no mandate to reform the social system of the South. However, under Thomas's encouragement, Dr. William Amberson of the University of Tennessee, completed a League for Industrial Democracy case study of over five hundred share-cropper families in Tennessee, Arkansas and Mississippi. Under the share system, the landlord furnishes the tenant farmer with a shack, tools and a mule and receives half of the proceeds from the produce of the land he works. There is no doubt that the share-cropper faces the same unfairness as the factory worker in the town where the company store operates. Landlords also have an agreement not to hire any share-cropper who is in debt to any other landlord. As it is estimated that at least 60 per cent of the cotton farmers are share-croppers, it is easy to see that a mere enhancement of

the price of cotton under the New Deal adjustment program cannot of itself insure better living conditions for the
mass of Southern farmers, especially when the higher
prices are achieved by a reduction of acreage in cotton.
And with the mechanical cotton-picker "just around the
corner," the dynamic possibilities of the Southern system
of land-tenure cannot be over-estimated.

In the "St. Louis Post-Dispatch" of March 11, 1934, the
following conditions were reported as typical:

The owner reserves the right to employ any extra labor
he deems necessary and charge it to the cropper's account.

The cropper agrees to furnish the necessary labor to keep
the ditches open, to pay ten cents per acre for maintaining
roads and ditches on the plantation, and to pay a supervision
and management fee, which custom has fixed as ten cents on
the dollar of advances at the store.

The Amberson Committee reported that the average income per year for the share-cropper and his entire working family was $262. Living conditions are dire in every
respect. Families live like animals in weird nests of tin
cans, canvas and old packing cases, and pellagra—that disease of malnutrition—is increasing. The Department of
Agriculture has taken cognizance of the situation, in the
gingerly manner enjoined by the political and social
T.N.T. involved, and the 1934–35 Cotton Acreage Reduction Contract states

(the planter) shall effect the acreage reduction as nearly rat-
able as practicable among tenants on this farm; shall, in so
far as possible, maintain on this farm the normal number of
tenants and other employees

and provides that the tenant shall receive one-half a cent
per pound for cotton not grown in 1934.

"In so far as possible" is a phrase through which any

plantation-owner can drive a team of mules. The Amberson report contends that "the acreage reduction program has operated to reduce the number of families in employment on cotton farms . . . due to . . . failure to reduce acreage ratably, forcing some tenants into the 'no-crop' class" and goes on to state that many of the tenants are forced into the day-labor class, with wages as low as 65 cents a day, and also that there is widespread replacement of white employees by colored help who accept a lower standard of living.

The loosely worded Cotton Reduction Contract, combined with inadequate enforcement of its provisions for agricultural labor, has created a group of restless, militant share-croppers who are responsive to the preachings of economic radicalism and are causing grave anxiety at Washington. For example, the Agricultural Adjustment Administration sent an investigator, Mrs. Mary Myers, to Marked Tree, Arkansas, to study the situation. Arkansas is the political bailiwick of Joe Robinson, Administration floor leader in the Senate. Her report has not been published.

Norman Thomas, in addition to his action in calling attention to the situation in the cotton belt, has intervened in the active politics of the South by promoting the Southern Tenant Farmers' Union in Eastern Arkansas. He has been energetic in the actual organization and has been assisted by several members of Commonwealth College, including Lucian Koch and Bob Reed. The Union, which claims a membership of over 5,000, is unique in the South in that it is bi-racial, having enlisted the cooperation of white and black share-croppers in one of the most significant developments on the agricultural labor front. Last March, Thomas made a tour of the East Arkansas cotton regions and was driven out of the town of

Birdsong and refused the right to hold a meeting in the public square at Marked Tree. (He later held the meeting from the porch of a private home there.) Senator Joseph T. Robinson of Arkansas had proposed dealing with the situation by permitting the share-croppers to acquire land by Federal loans, but Thomas wired Joe, "There will probably be massacre long before your plan of rural rehabilitation can be started."

Nevertheless, the leaders of Southern Democracy at Washington are following the land-purchase method of dealing with the cropper problem. The Bankhead Bill proposes that a Farm Tenant Corporation be formed, with a capital of $100,000,000 and the power to issue one billion dollars worth of bonds. The cropper is to be entitled to buy a farm at the unit price of $2,000. His cotton crop at current price-levels would sell for $200, out of which interest and amortization charges of $80 a year would be deducted. This would leave him with an income of $120 a year, from which to pay taxes and production costs before clothing, feeding and educating his family. With the tendency toward cheap day labor, and the company or landowner store, the Bankhead system would probably leave him better off and more secure than he is under the present system of peonage, but Norman Thomas says that the Bankhead Bill is totally inadequate and that, if it passes, he will continue his agitation in the Tenants' Union.

The situation is already becoming an acute political issue, and Governor Futrell of Arkansas has refused to have temporary refugee camps for evicted share-croppers, while the A.A.A. at Washington has not seen its way to dealing with the evicted farmers by establishing colonies on the government-rented lands. So the cropper problem promises to become one of the most disturbing and dangerous problems of the agricultural front and of the South, where economic, social and political reform is long over-due. Norman Thomas thus finds himself in on the ground floor in the organization of justified discontent against these intolerable conditions. In this he has stolen a march on the Communists who, though active in the South, think largely in terms of the industrial "proletariat" and of arousing the negroes to revolutionary action. Thomas, on the other hand, has been successful in enrolling negro clergymen in active service in the Tenants' Union, and the Reverend A. Brooking, negro organizer for the croppers, had revolver shots fired around his home last March as a protest against his "revolutionary" activities.

The materials of a social war are banking up in the cotton belt, as a result, and the Arkansas planters have started a "company union," the Marked Tree Coöperative Association, membership in which is limited to white share-croppers. So far it has met with scant success, but the political machinery is distinctly in the hands of the planters. The croppers are caught between the cotton-reduction program of the Triple-A and the State administration of the F.E.R.A., and the Arkansas Relief Director is a planter. The truth is, of course, that if the Tenants' Union actually makes material headway throughout the South, a determined though somewhat sub-conscious effort will be made to divert its threat of social war into the old Southern channel of race-hatred, and to save the Southern system by playing off the poor whites against the blacks. In these circumstances, the question arises whether Norman Thomas is a sufficiently astute politician to direct the storm his propaganda is helping to create. It seems extremely doubtful.

III

It is significant that the change of American Socialism from a minority political party, such as it was under Gene Debs, to a radical political propaganda group under Norman Thomas, should have passed unnoticed by the bulk of observers.

This is because the Socialist Party still goes through the motions of party politics and because its leader underscores his sermons to American capitalists by running for office with a uniform lack of success that ought to have suggested the truth long ago: namely, that Socialist Party politics have become simple publicity stunts to win attention to Socialist ideas and that, far from being discredited by defeat, the Party leaders thrive on it. Victory would be the only thing which could expose their game as being an ingenious adaptation of Marxian dogma to the practice of American pressure-politics.

Thomas has run for Congressman, Governor of New York (1924), Mayor of New York City (1925 and 1929), and President of the United States (1928 and 1932). His best showing was for Mayor in 1929, when he got 175,000 votes, as "silk-stocking" Republicans, including many bankers and corporation lawyers, voted for him because they couldn't stand the proletarian uncouthness of the Republican candidate, Fiorello H. LaGuardia, who was beaten by Jimmy Walker in Tammany's most costly victory of the present century.

Although Thomas does not appear to understand fully the true function of American Socialism, he has opposed united fronts with other groups, instinctively, as being calculated to impair Socialism's value as propaganda, but he sees that it is quite possible that in 1940, if not 1936, a Third Party may be organized with a virtual Socialist platform. The Farmer-Labor platform of 1934 was an almost exact parallel to the Socialist platform of 1932 but such is the pig-headed dogmatism of most American radicals that the Socialists will probably attack their own program as "Fascist" if it is sponsored by another group. Moreover, as dissenters from Marx on some points of theory and as sturdy believers in democratic policies and methods of government, the Socialists find it difficult to reach a common front with the Communists, although they now have a special committee, appointed by the Party Congress this March in Buffalo, to look into the whole problem of radical hook-ups.

All that the Socialists have to contribute to a Third Party movement is a demonstration of successful municipal government in Milwaukee, the respectability and fluent pen and tongue of Norman Thomas, and an inherent ability to engage in abstruse doctrinal controversies until half-past Armageddon. There is one exception to be noted against this political weakness: the possibility that they may exploit and develop their new field for agitation at the bottom of the share-cropper situation in the South. But that, it is likely, will be stolen from them by either Long or the Communists, who are also very active in the South, and in any case, any effective work for the share-croppers will take the form of a social revolution in the South and will produce the old crop of night-riders, Ku Kluxers, Vigilantes, lynchers, and government by deputy sheriff, which might discredit Socialism as an effective political force and weaken its value as a campaign to educate Americans in the possibilities of economic brotherhood.

In the meantime, Thomas is playing his cards carefully. Although he has consented to examine the possibility of collaboration with the Communists, he has nothing to gain from normal political opportunism. His Party's present stand contemplates a drive against the sales tax, in favor of increased income and inheritance taxes, and support of the thirty-hour week. He has no patience with the panacea peddlers and has denounced Coughlin, Townsend and Utopia, Inc., as "Fascist in spirit but transient and futile and based on the puerile and impossible economics of the New Deal." He also does not go along with the advocates of a Third Party movement, feeling that it is not very strong or very popular, and being chiefly anxious that Long, whom he regards as a thorough Fascist, should not grab off the Third Party leadership, although he is well-disposed to a Farmer-Labor movement with a Socialist platform. On this account, therefore, Thomas will be more apt to continue the political status quo, with Roosevelt taking the responsibility for economic and social transition and the Rev. Norman Mattoon Thomas using the Socialist Party platform as a means of supplying the New Deal with its specific policies. It is a situation which would make Marx turn in his grave and which causes bitter teeth-gnashing in Moscow, but it conforms to the essential guts of American politics and is probably the best and quickest way available for the orderly change of American institutions away from individual competition and toward the new ideal of social coöperation—new, that is, to Americans.

X

SWEET FASCISM IN THE PINEY WOODS

IT SHOULD BE a constant source of amazement to foreign observers that Americans, while proudly insisting that Fascism is un-American and must never be permitted to find a foothold in the United States, consistently ignore the fact that the long-leaf pine and pellagra belt which stretches from the Potomac to the Gulf of Mexico and from the Atlantic to the Mississippi River has been governed by Fascist methods since 1876.

All of the stigmata of European Fascism are there—though none of the glory. There is Government by a single political party—the Democratic instead of the Nazis or the Fascisti; there is coercion and terrorization of the opposition and minority by armed bands of licensed bullies—Ku Kluxers, night-riders, lynching mobs instead of Storm-Troopers and Squadristi; there is of course the issue of racial supremacy and the proscription of a subject race—Negro instead of Jewish—with respect not only to public office and economic power but also with respect to culture and marriage; there is the rigid regimentation of the individual in matters of opinion and conscience, as witnessed by Tennessee's "monkey-law" and the short shrift given Northern investigators into social conditions, and there is the effective dragooning of organized labor by deputy sheriffs, militia and legislation.

Students of current trends in Europe could do far worse

than study the revolution led by the lower middle class in the South after the plantation-owners had been discredited by their defeat in the Civil War, and their establishment of a crystallized Fascist type of civilization south of the Mason-Dixon line. Here and there the South is beginning to stir under the iron grip of this "bourgeois" dictatorship, allied as in Europe with powerful corporations, but generally *de facto* Fascism still reigns in the piney woods and offers the most determined resistance to the reforms and reconstruction proffered by the New Deal.

When the right of labor to strike and to engage in peaceful picketing is regarded as "revolution," when the right of labor to organize is regarded as "Socialism," when the right of free intellectual inquiry into the character of economic institutions and the value of social relationships is punished as "radicalism," what chance has Norman Thomas of getting far with his union of white and colored share-croppers? Yet until the South responds to the new social and economic forces which have been unleashed by the World War and by the post-war industrial revolution, the entire nation will be handicapped. There are more and more Southerners who realize this fact and are endeavoring to meet it, and all is far from black in the black belt. Yet Southern politics remains essentially Fascist in tone. The Democratic Party nomination is the equivalent to election and the Supreme Court has recently ruled, in a Texas case, that the Democratic Party can confine itself to lily-white membership.

The work of the Civil War still stands and the small farmer and the poor whites still rule—an interesting commentary upon the popularly held theory that this nation's problems can be solved only if we break up the urban conglomerations and return the population to a life on small farms. A small gallery of Southern politicians suggests the plane of statesmanship which can be supported by such a type of civilization. It also suggests that the South itself is slowly shedding its Fascist institutions and may become spiritually reunited to the rest of the country.

II

In Eugene Talmadge, Governor of Georgia, we confront the Solid South at its solidest. Talmadge has created more of an uproar than any Governor south of the Mason-Dixon line in the last eighteen months. His trumpeted attacks on the Roosevelt Administration and on most of the things it stands for have attracted the favorable attention of conservatives in the South—and elsewhere— who are looking for a "safe" "man of the people" to save them from both Roosevelt and Long. From the Tory point of view, there is no appreciable difference between the New Deal and Share-Our-Wealth. Both are "Socialistic."

The Georgia Fuehrer has the following achievements emblazoned in his record:

He "kept the rails hot" riding to Washington to shake down all the Federal agencies with relief or other money at their disposal. The plight of the State of Georgia, as he pictured it, was beyond human comprehension, but, as the money began to roll in, in response to his impassioned pleas, he promptly reduced expenditures by the State government, thus making himself a great "economy" hero. He followed this by upbraiding the Federal Government (which was paying the sums he was saving the Georgia tax-payers) for its "extravagance," presenting himself as a man who knew how to cut taxes in the depression. Of course, the Federal Government could call his hand by shutting off relief funds, but it has so far considered the welfare of the Georgia underdogs as more important than Georgia's naive backwoods Fascism. Accordingly, the Federal Government has kept Georgia's schools open, has carried most of the State's relief burden and is generally, by roads, and other P.W.A. projects, reconstructing the State—while Talmadge takes the credit.

He has adopted a violently anti-labor policy and, in the fall of 1934, displayed an effective technique in cracking-down on a textile strike. He turned out forty National Guard companies who seized 200 strike-pickets and herded them into a detention camp near Atlanta—*à la* Hitler—without trial or law. The troops arrested other strikers, about 130 in a single town, and later in the fall used the same tactics to break up a hosiery mill strike at Rossville.

Talmadge showed that he knew what he was doing and that there was no pretense that the detention camps were needed to preserve law and order, by his statement at the time of the textile strike: "When any citizen of Georgia wants to work, they have an unalienable right, under the Constitution, to do so. I do not want anyone in Georgia interfering with those who want to work and I have notified the Adjutant General to carry out these principles."

"The Manufacturers Record" was so delighted with this evidence of right-mindedness that it invited him to write an article for this hundred per cent open-shop minded publication, in which Talmadge said, "When anyone quits a job, he does not have the right to hang around the place of business and interfere with anyone else who wants to work on the job."

William Green of the A. F. of L. and various liberals protested in vain. Talmadge called the A. F. of L. leaders "loafers and bluffers," adding that "the men and women of America are not going to be bulldozed by any such persons." There was joy in the Chambers of Commerce and other conventicles of the Old Religion—at last they had found a man who dared stand up for capital and to hell with labor, although they had had to go far afield to find him.

Very far afield. Talmadge was born in the little village of Forsyth, Georgia, on September 23, 1884, the year Grover Cleveland was first elected as the first Democratic President since the Civil War. Talmadge got a law degree from the University of Georgia at the age of twenty-three and set up practice in the little town of McRae. He was solicitor of the city court for two years and then attorney for Telfair County for three years. In 1927, he was elected Commissioner of Agriculture—a job he held until the New Deal election of 1932. In that year he won the gubernatorial nomination from a field of six candidates and was, of course, elected. He was renominated and reëlected in 1934.

Talmadge owed his first nomination to the Georgia "rotten borough" system (though other States have similar devices), under which three counties, with less than a thousand voters each, cast as many votes as does the City of Atlanta in a Democratic primary. Under this unit-voting system—which also applies to the Legislature—the poorest and least populated of Georgia's 150 counties are enabled to control the entire State. In 1932, for example, Talmadge polled only 116,000 out of 292,000 votes in the primary, but had a clear majority—252 out of 410—of the "unit" votes. One understands better the affiliation between Tammany and the Solid South. In 1934, on the other hand, Talmadge carried all but three counties.

The viciousness of this system is accentuated by the fact that Georgia has been going industrial steadily, while Talmadge represents the point of view of the poor white farmer on the marginal edge of cotton production, not the share-cropper, but the small landowner and the fellow who hires a few share-croppers—what the French, in their candor, would call the peasantry. Talmadge represents the peasant stinginess, shrewdness, ignorance and prejudice of the pathetic figure near the bottom of the social scramble who has nobody to look down upon but the still more pathetic but happy-go-lucky negroes.

Talmadge is, of course, of somewhat higher status, being the Georgian equivalent of a Calvin Coolidge. He went to college and got a law degree, though he does his best to overcome that handicap. He married a moderately wealthy widow and promptly moved to her farm and in his Who's Who biography remarks, "actively engaged in farming since 1912." He is swarthy in appearance, of medium build and bespectacled, and affects red suspenders and shirt-sleeves when he is out on the stump. In the Governor's office he is ordinarily well-dressed and comports himself according to the amenities.

As Commissioner of Agriculture he held the headlines of the weekly papers by his attacks on the "Fertilizer Trust" and forced the fertilizer companies to make rebates whenever their products fell below the specified ingredients. He also made the conventional economy gesture—dropping people from the payroll. When he ran for Governor it was on a simple program shrewdly gauged to the narrow horizons of the struggling Georgia small property owner: Reduce the property tax by 20 per cent; lower the license fees for automobiles; compel the public utilities to reduce rates; take the highway department "out of the hands of the politicians and return it to the people."

He has kept all of his promises, except the one about the highway department. He cut license fees to $3 per car

—and to do it he had to battle with the Legislature, remove the State Motor Vehicle Commissioner, and rely on a statute passed in 1821, empowering the Governor to suspend any or part of any tax measure. Despite this important loss of revenue he cut the property tax 20 per cent. To a man owning a farm assessed at $1,000, that meant saving $1 a year, but $1 a year is carefully counted among the people who vote for Talmadge—and it is estimated that the average annual saving per farmer under this reduction was 53 cents. The people who were saved enormous amounts were the big property-owners—and especially the railroads, electric and other utilities. With this saving they could easily afford to accede to part of his demands for lower rates to the consumers. Even so, Talmadge had to go through a real fight with these corporations to get them to pass on any part of the saving to the public. He kicked out the Public Service Commission and appointed a new one and finally threatened to raise the assessed valuation of utility properties to the value claimed by them as a basis for rate-making. Since that would have more than wiped out their saving from the property tax reduction, he got his way. After several court fights, the railroads, the electrical utilities, the telephone companies, and the gas companies finally gave in and reduced their charges substantially.

So much to his credit. Mussolini got the trains to run on time. Talmadge's highway reform was not so impressive. Talmadge got control of the department, all right, and a good many of his relatives and friends landed on the payroll. Nothing more was done about returning it "to the people"—and nothing more was necessary. He tried to control the relief organization but Harry Hopkins soon took it out from under him and announced to all and sundry that the "Cowboy Governor" of Georgia would have no further connection with C.W.A., F.E.R.A. or any similar enterprise. Instead, Hopkins put in charge Miss Gay Shepperson, a very efficient woman, who has made Georgia relief work a model in many respects.

It is not a model so far as the State's contributions are concerned. It is almost entirely Federal-supported relief. Some of the counties chipped in, but for two years the State gave not one red cent for the relief of its own people until last winter the Federal Government was directly supporting almost 500,000 of Georgia's 2,800,000 inhabitants. Meanwhile, Talmadge has continued to whittle down state expenditures. He tried to close the School of Journalism at the University of Georgia and he squeezed the schools. He also reduced the cost of administering the State's penal system by pardoning or paroling more than 1,000 prisoners, in his first year and a half of office.

His renomination in 1934 was due to the support of Clark Howell, editor of "The Atlanta Constitution," who for ten years has carried on a bitter political feud with Major John S. Cohen, editor of "The Atlanta Journal." Both Howell and Cohen were among the earliest supporters of F.D.R., but the State platform adopted under Talmadge's guidance was a direct attack on the New Deal. Republican editors gleefully published extracts of it from one end of the country to the other—for here were well-deserving Democrats who had out-Liberty-Leagued the Liberty League—and predicted that the Democratic Party would split if Roosevelt continued on his "mad course of socialism." In this connection, Talmadge had denounced the N.R.A. and was the first Governor to protest against the minimum wage rates established by the C.W.A. Harry Hopkins was forced to back down on this point for, low as the C.W.A. wages were, they were high enough to take the negro laborers away from their pre-

scribed duties and ruin the labor market for the small
Georgia farmer.

The Howell-Talmadge combination followed the attack on the New Deal by booting out Major Cohen to
make room for a new National Democratic Committeeman. There was some doubt about the legality of this,
and Jim Farley took the position that Cohen was still
National Committeeman from Georgia. The Howell-
Talmadge combination held out against Cohen all right
—but it couldn't hold out against Talmadge. In April,
1935, the "Cowboy Governor" took a step farther in his
attack on the New Deal and assailed Roosevelt, with a
reference to his physical handicap. This was too much for
Howell, who promptly threw Talmadge overboard. Talmadge, apparently undisturbed, went right on with his
attacks, but the loss of Howell was a serious blow to his
program to run against Roosevelt in the Georgia Presidential primaries.

Talmadge is not a potential leader of national Fascism,
as successful Fascist leaders usually remain radical until
they get into power. Talmadge has all the power he can
use and has already shown his hand in his symbolism of
the alliance of the small property-owner with the road-
contractor and the mill-owner against factory labor, farm
labor and the wretched share-cropper. Talmadge is, however, somewhat more dangerous than is Huey Long in his
own small way. It is practically assured that the old-style
Southern set-up will use Talmadge to fight Long, unless
Talmadge suddenly sees that there are more votes to be
had by trailing with Long. It would not be impossible
for him to swing over to a "Share-Our-Wealth" movement
which, under the Kingfish's Plan, would hit only the
multi-millionaires and leave untouched Georgia's cotton
mill-owners—with their militia, their stretch-outs and

their open shop principles. However, Long has gone pro-labor and it would be difficult for Talmadge to do the same, after his detention camps and his cracks at the Federation leaders. Still, anything is possible among the Georgia electorate for a man who knows the "cracker" psychology and can make the rotten-borough unit-vote system work for him against most popular majorities.

III

Allied in function to Talmadge, is Theodore Gilmore Bilbo, Junior Senator from Mississippi and one of the South's best-established rabble-rousers.

For more than a generation "the man Bilbo" has had a stranglehold on the small farmer vote of Mississippi. Born fifty-eight years ago in Juniper Grove, Mississippi, Bilbo studied at the University of Nashville for three years, dropped out for several years of teaching country schools, and then studied law at Vanderbilt and Michigan Universities. He then simultaneously entered the practice of law and politics—the two things are synonymous in rural America—at Poplarsville, Mississippi. He followed the smoothly-worn *cursus honorum* of Democratic machine-politics in the cotton belt, first to the State Senate, then to the Lieutenant-Governorship (1912–16) and finally to the Governorship (1916–20). He stepped out for a term, as is required by the constitutions of many Southern States, and was beaten for the gubernatorial nomination in 1924 by the women, whose enfranchisement he had neglected to espouse. By 1928 he had been sufficiently forgiven to win the second term as Governor, and in 1934 he went after the nomination for the United States Senate.

It was a three-cornered race, the progressive Representative Ross Collins and Senator Hubert Stephens being the other entries. When no one got a majority in the first primary, Collins, who was low man, dropped out, and Bilbo nosed out Stephens in the run-off primary, thus bringing to an end a career of unterrified but undistinguished Tory Democracy in the Senate.

Bilbo is a typical spell-binder from the Deep South who once called Senator Stephens "a vicious, malicious, pusillanimous, cold-blooded, premeditated, plain, ordinary United States Senatorial liar." That kind of talk packs 'em in the aisle in the Southern camp-meeting belt. In fact, Bilbo has the true camp-meeting touch. As a young man he learned to play an organ and sing hymns, and these talents became a stock part of his electioneering technique, since many Mississippi campaign meetings are held in churches—they have the only halls in the average country district. At Poplarsville, Bilbo took the precaution of becoming secretary of the County Baptist Association and frequently substituted for the pastor in rural Baptist churches.

It would be stupid to pretend that men like Bilbo are mere slick electioneers, or even inherently conservative when measured against their State psychology. As a matter of record, Bilbo put through some highly progressive measures in his first term as Governor, such as establishing a State tubercular hospital and a school for delinquent minors, improving the penal system and refurbishing the old capitol. He couldn't succeed himself under Mississippi law, but he elected one of his friends to the job. This friend, Lee Russell, was sued for breach of promise by a stenographer. Bilbo refused to testify for the stenographer and was jailed for contempt of court—not his first brush with the law. As a State Senator he took money to vote for a candidate for the United States Senate. He said

—in fact, announced—that he took it to trap the bribers, and produced evidence that he had discussed it with his friends beforehand, but he escaped impeachment by only one vote. He is not the type of person who makes money out of politics. He has always been near the subsistence level in public life.

Bilbo's second term as Governor produced little but oratory and one deadlock after another with the Legislature. His program was constructive: a brick highway system built by convict labor, a State printing plant to print free text books for the schools, consolidation of rural schools, creation of a State constabulary, and such. He was blocked at every turn, but his successor took over much of the program and put it across—and also strove valiantly to clean up the financial mess which Bilbo had left behind through failure to tax properly.

Perhaps the chief difference between Bilbo and Long is that Long had the cleverness and ruthlessness to put over his program and get a political grip on his State, while Bilbo could get elected but lacked the capacity to handle a legislature and cement his political power.

When Roosevelt came into power at Washington, Bilbo was badly in need of a job and Senator Stephens, Bilbo's bitter enemy, wouldn't help him. At this point, Pat Harrison, the good-natured, conservative Democratic stalwart, gave him a lift. Bilbo was placed in the Agricultural Adjustment Administration as chief of its press clipping service at a salary of $6,000. The following year, Bilbo went back to take his revenge on Stephens, who had been in the Senate since 1923. Pat Harrison was on the spot. Harrison's term expires in 1936 and he had viewed with anxious concern the rise of the Kingfish just across the line in Louisiana and the spread of his Share-Our-Wealth movement in Mississippi. Pat went through the gestures of helping Stephens but saw to it that he didn't make an enemy of Bilbo.

It was a red-hot campaign. Bilbo made more than a thousand speeches, and he draws a big crowd whenever he speaks. The Mississippi farmers like his style—his medium build, his pinched Coolidgean face, his sporty clothes and his spread-eagle oratory. Bilbo based his campaign on a promise to "out-Huey Huey" when he got to the Senate—and the crowds ate it up, which is no mean compliment to the Senator from Louisiana. However, Bilbo was too cautious to make a direct hook-up with the Kingfish. The Long crowd wanted to come into Mississippi for the run-off and help him—on condition. Bilbo shied at the condition. Two or three days before the votes were cast, according to the Kingfish crowd, Bilbo telephoned Huey asking him to instruct the Share-Our-Wealth Clubs (who had supported Collins in the primary, but without open direction from Long) to vote for him. Long replied that he would send telegrams at his own expense to all the Share-Our-Wealth Clubs in Mississippi, urging them to vote for Bilbo, if Bilbo would send a telegram asking him to do so and promising to support the Share-Our-Wealth program. Bilbo sent an evasive reply but probably got most of the Share-Our-Wealth votes anyway.

When Bilbo strode into the Senate on his pledge to "out-Huey Huey" there were rumbles of delighted anticipation, but the word soon came that Pat Harrison had this "wild man" in hand and, sure enough, one fine day Pat turned up at the White House with Bilbo in tow. And Bilbo came out of the White House and announced that he would go down the line for the New Deal. As a reward, he got better committee assignments than usually fall to Senatorial "freshmen" and doubtless assurance of a bigger share of patronage than generally comes the way of a Junior Senator from a "sure" State.

Then the word spread that, under Pat's management, Bilbo was primed to "take on" the Kingfish at the very outset of the 1935 session of Congress. He was to be the man who gave Huey a dose of his own medicine and the "insiders" waited for the fireworks—but in vain. When Long speaks, Bilbo is always there, watching like a hawk. Sometimes he moves up in a front seat to get a better view of Huey in action, but he has not yet "taken him on." Perhaps, after hearing Huey's oratorical orgasms, Bilbo decided that discretion is the better part of politics when faced with your superior in the art of rough-and-tumble debate. Perhaps Pat has decided that it is better strategy not to fire until you see the whites of their eyes.

As matters stand, Bilbo is the man who may save Pat Harrison his Senate seat in 1936. Long is camping on Pat's trail and if Long could find a good candidate to put up against him, Pat would have tough sledding in 1936, just as Joe Robinson is likely to have, and for the same reason. However, if Bilbo remains loyal to Pat, the Long invasion will be met at the border by the veteran adjective-stringer of Poplarsville. The Long people are already preparing for the battle. They have combed Bilbo's variegated history and will try to pillory him, and if the Long people don't back down and if Bilbo doesn't change his spots, the Senatorial primary in Mississippi in 1936 may be one of the most glorious oratorical and mud-slinging free-for-alls in recent political history.

The significance of this battle is not in Bilbo's personality but in the fact that it may be the opening gun in Long's campaign to strike at Roosevelt by enlarging the Kingfish Empire in the Deep South and by punishing one

rate from typhoid fever being cut in half, while tuberculosis declined and small-pox and dysentery practically disappeared.

This was an elementary job, but many of the South's political problems are elementary problems as compared to those of the Northern industrial States, and Graves seems to have done the job well. The law of Alabama forbade him to succeed himself but he came back in 1934 and once more won the nomination for the Governorship. This time he ran as an out-and-out New Dealer, pledged to the Federal Child Labor Amendment, the establishment of a State Department of Labor, old age pensions, unemployment insurance, better regulation of public utilities, coöperation with T.V.A., and similar reforms. His Klan days were forgotten and liberals and labor rallied to his support.

Bibb Graves thus appears to be a subtler, but more effective, way of counteracting the Long influence than that represented by Bilbo. It should not be forgotten that the Kingfish, notwithstanding his clamor for wealth-sharing, has done virtually nothing in the way of even elementary social security legislation. Moreover, Graves does not represent the old-style upper-class Southern politician whom Huey has been lashing with whips of scorpions in New Orleans. He was born in Hope Hull, Alabama, in 1873, graduated from the University of Alabama in 1893 and from Yale Law School in 1896. He took up law practice in Montgomery, served two terms in the State Legislature, and was City Attorney and Democratic State Chairman before he won the nomination for Governor in 1926. Moreover, unlike the Kingfish, he did not avoid the Army during the World War. Instead, he served in the National Guard since his youth, went to France as Colonel of the 117th Field Artillery, and helped to organize the Alabama command of the American Legion.

Graves, together with the leaders of the Alabama delegation in Congress—the liberal Hugh Black and the intelligent Bankhead brothers—represents the wiser and more responsible elements in the Deep South. They realize that the old order is changing, that the South has been backward in its social legislation, and that it must readjust itself to cope with the rise of industrialism—Birmingham, Alabama, is potentially the iron capital of North America—and with the dubious future of cotton. In the last two years, Alabama has led all other States in the active rehabilitation of landless farmers—dispossessed small owners, tenants and share-croppers—by placing them on small pieces of land. Senator Bankhead is now sponsoring the broad plan to expand and improve this method of rehabilitation throughout the South and the entire country.

The importance of Bibb Graves in this process is that he knows how to appeal to the Alabama back-countrymen. As a rabble-rouser he is no match for Long, Talmadge or Bilbo, but Alabama is a responsible and conservative community and the process of moderate change which her leaders have initiated is an ameliorating force in the social struggle that is coming to the surface in the South. This struggle is an intensely serious element in the national picture—Long and his rivals are exploiting the grievances which make it inevitable, where people like Graves and Johnston of South Carolina are striving to remove the cause of those grievances by progressive legislation.

For the South may have had its Tom Heflins and its Coley Bleases—just as Georgia now has its Talmadge—but in South Carolina last fall something new happened under the Southern sun. A former cotton mill-hand was elected Governor, when Olin D. Johnston beat Coleman

L. Blease in the primary and on January 5, 1935, took the oath of office at the State House in Columbia.

Industrialism has spread so rapidly through the Piedmont area that today there are about 60,000 cotton mill-hands in South Carolina, and they account for a fifth of the vote, but never until last year did they nominate one of their own for a major office. Last year, they lost their old poor-white consciousness and to a certain extent began to vote according to their interests as mill-workers rather than according to their prejudice as former agrarians.

Johnston's story is typical of what has been happening to the poor whites in the Southern Piedmont. He was the son of a poor farmer. At the age of twelve he went to work in a mill in the village of Honea Path, later the scene of some savage fighting during the textile strike of 1934. He worked his way through the Textile Institute at Spartanburg and then through two years at Wofford College, supporting himself by pressing pants in the daytime and reading proof on a local newspaper at night. When we entered the World War, he volunteered, went to Europe with the A.E.F., and returned after the armistice with the chevrons of a sergeant and a citation for bravery in action.

He then finished his course at Wofford and got a law degree at the University of South Carolina, opening a law office in Spartanburg. While he was still at college he was elected to the State Legislature and he was reëlected when he took up law practice. In 1930, he entered the race for the Governorship. Starting as a dark horse, he led the first primary and was beaten by a narrow margin in the run-off. During the next four years he visited every corner of the State, developed a good platform manner, and prepared for his next campaign. In 1934 he ran again and was elected.

In contrast to some Southern demagogues who affect

the shirt-sleeves, tobacco-chawing, call-me-Charley technique of hobnobbing with the voters, Johnston showed
himself as a pleasant but a dignified man, who knew how
to speak literate English and was not afraid to show signs
of ordinary intelligence on a higher than a mule's rump
level. He didn't need to remind the farmers and the mill-
hands that he was one of them. They knew it and they
also liked oracular proof that one of themselves could
become as personable, intelligent and important as any
gentleman born to wealth or privilege. Johnston won the
1934 run-off primary, and with it the election, as a real
representative of the South which is shaking off the poor-
white complex.

He ran as a moderate liberal, Roosevelt style, and as
in most Southern States one of his big cards was a pledge
to reduce the auto license tax. South Carolina has been
a poverty-stricken State since the northern victory in the
Civil War diverted to New York the railway traffic which
had made Charleston the greatest port of shipment in
the United States, and it has not produced any dynamic
political figures since the age of Calhoun and the statesmen of secession. On this account, Johnston is being carefully watched. He is neither a rabble-rouser nor a reactionary, but probably belongs to the same category as
Bibb Graves of Alabama, although as yet he is unproved.

His importance lies in what he symbolizes, rather than
in his own political motive power. A powerful process is
at work throughout the South, and even in parts of the
industrial North and East, to substitute the rule of farmers
and laborers for government by remote control of bankers
and business men. The instrument of that remote control
has been, in the South, the careful cultivation of prejudice, against the negro or against the North, rather than
against a system by which such prejudices could be in-

voked as a device to prevent economic reform or social justice from interfering with irresponsible profiteering.

The development in South Carolina is also worth noticing because of the very great influence of Mr. Bernard M. Baruch in this, his native State, as well as in other areas within the range of the Kingfish. While some nonsense has been spread as to the extent and character of Baruch's grip on Southern Democratic politics, it is no secret that Long is fighting Baruch and it is logical to assume that Baruch is fighting back. The question remains as to Baruch's choice of weapons. Do Talmadge and Bilbo represent the means by which the major speculative and financial forces in Southern politics are attempting to combat the "Share-Our-Wealth" movement or is their answer to be moderate and less dramatic reformers of the caliber of Graves and Johnston?

The answer to this question is one that concerns the entire country, for it alone can supply the final explanation to what has been happening in regions closer to the seat of the American financial empire than the squalid mill towns of the Piedmont and the tax-ridden poor farmers of the lower reaches of the Mississippi.

XI

DISQUIET ON THE EASTERN FRONT

BROADLY SPEAKING, the means by which the business and financial interests which are summed up in the expression "Wall Street" have ruled the nation since the Civil War, have been to play off the West against the South. To do so implied their firm control of the Northeastern area— that vital quadrangle between the Potomac and Ohio Rivers, the Great Lakes and the Atlantic Ocean. The old Jacksonian Democracy—as prepared by Jefferson—ruled the Northeastern States by an alliance of the West and South which persisted down to the Civil War. The Republicans lured the West away from the South by the promise of free lands to the pioneers and since then have retained, with brief interludes, a Western allegiance which is partly based on gratitude for this past favor and partly on the memory of the four years' struggle to overthrow the slave power and maintain an outlet to the sea down the Mississippi River.

The most suggestive feature of present-day politics is, not the temporary alliance of the West and South which is the political basis for the policies of the New Deal, but the success of the progressive policies thereby engendered in splitting the East itself and carrying the social war into the Holy of Holies of American industrial capitalism.

If there are three localities where this capitalistic imperialism has been paramount it is in the Allegheny coal-fields of Pennsylvania and West Virginia, in New York City and in Massachusetts. It was Massachusetts which fought and won the war against the South (with the aid of the rest of the Northern States, to be sure, but the policy was supplied by Massachusetts). It was West Virginia which became a conquered province, torn away from the Southern Confederacy, and established as a community in which the great corporations could run wild. It was New York City which provided the most suitable administrative capital for this new economic empire created on the ruins of the conquered South and the deluded West.

Boston, New York and Pittsburgh became the real seats of American power after Appomattox and have continued to exercise imperial influence in all but name ever since: Pittsburgh as the capital of iron, coal, oil and gas; New York as the capital of money and commerce and shipping; Boston as the intellectual capital, with colonies stretching up into the Maritime Provinces of Canada and down to the West Indies and Central America. These three, with their political hinterlands, were the rulers of America. Now they are losing the allegiance of their own citizens—perhaps only for the moment—to the New Deal. For the East is beaten, morally, and is capable of supplying no further leadership, only craftiness. Its "radical" groups are the tail to any man's kite but have no lifting capacity of their own. Their defection from the rule of Wall Street symbolizes the end of a political era and must be considered in the light of a last minute rush for the bandwagon.

II

Two conspicuous events in the 1934 election had an important common factor. They were the Democratic victory in Pennsylvania—the election of a Governor and a Senator in the traditional rock-ribbed home of Joe Grundy—and the election of Rush D. Holt, aged twenty-nine, on the Democratic ticket in Messrs. Mellon's and Rockefeller's business backyard of West Virginia. The common factor in both of these phenomena was the resurrection of the United Mine Workers under John L. Lewis and their effective seizure of political power. The mine workers alone were not responsible for the result in either case, but their influence was vital. The Pennsylvania Democrats saw the point and put an official of the U.M.W. on their ticket as candidate for Lieutenant-Governor. In West Virginia, the miners were the chief political element behind young Holt.

So far as the social background of the situation is concerned, suffice it to say that coal-mining, in addition to being a "sick industry" and greatly overmanned in relation to consumptive demand, has suffered the blessings of an irresponsible and absentee control, exercised by the steel industry, the banks and the railways, to an extent which has made the Pennsylvania and West Virginia coal-fields (the two are continuous) one of the most depressing problem-areas of the United States. The old story: low wages, unsanitary housing, disease, malnutrition, unemployment, strikes, deputy sheriffs, and "rugged individualism"—and enough of them to bank up bitter and ingrained resentment.

Although Rush Holt is not a miner, his sudden rise in the capitalistic province of West Virginia is a significant omen of the trend of the times. In a much more practical way than the Utopians, he is a product of Edward Bellamy's "Looking Backward" and the literature of early post-Civil War revolt. His father, Dr. Matthew Holt (now aged 84) ran away to join the Union Army at the age of thirteen but was hauled back by his father and later went to medical school, settling down as a general practitioner in the town of Weston, near Charleston, West Virginia. Dr. Holt, in addition to possessing tremendous vitality and a generous soul, also had a strong social conscience. He edited a Republican paper for a time but eventually turned Socialist, running once for Governor and twice for Senator on the Socialist ticket.

Dr. Holt was never elected to any office until, at the age of 82, he decided to run for Mayor of Weston. The "regular" machines ruled his name off the printed ballots but he ran anyway. The voters had to write in his name but they gave him more votes than they gave to the Democrat and the Republican combined, and he is still Mayor of Weston.

The doctor did not marry until he was forty-eight years old and Rush is the fourth of five children. At the age of fourteen he finished high school and tried to enter the University of Cincinnati but they wouldn't take him so he returned and went to the University of West Virginia. Later he switched to Salem College—one of those tiny denominational colleges which stud the hills of West Virginia—which gave him his A.B. degree. He taught for a couple of years and then returned to live with his family at Weston, where he helped run the family store and meat shop. He established his library in a small room above the shop and devoted himself to the study of public questions, especially to public utility legislation, between the cleaver and the ice-box, until in 1930 he felt competent to run for the West Virginia House of Delegates. He was elected and he was twenty-five years old.

Two days after he took his seat, he made his maiden speech and spoke again frequently throughout the session of the Legislature. His favorite topic was the regulation of public utilities and he knew more about it than anyone who dared take the floor against him in this, a utility-controlled State. During the next three years he made sensational legislative history. He attacked "absentee landlords" and "invisible government"; he drove through a resolution to investigate the large public utility corporations; he fought the sales tax unsuccessfully but forced higher taxes on the utilities; he fought political privilege and at one time blocked a compromise which would have permitted sheriffs to retain their ancient right to profiteer on the food supplied to prisoners. "Making profits on human misery is wrong and I will not compromise," he announced. What wonder that the Governor later besought him to keep "his unholy hands" off the Legislature when the State set up a Planning Council to act as funnel for Federal relief and rehabilitation funds.

As a legislator, Holt forced through the House of Delegates many progressive bills which were easily blocked in the State Senate by the interests which had become used to running the State, so he decided that he would have to continue the fight on a higher plane and went after the nomination for the U. S. Senate in 1934. He faced the regular Democratic machine and its chief factions, as well as all the vested interests of the State. Jim Farley backed Clem Shaver, former chairman of the Democratic National Committee in the days when the Democratic Party went dutifully to Wall Street for its candidates. Holt had the backing of the newly reorganized and militant United Mine Workers. It was enough. In the primary he beat nine candidates, six of whom were important, getting 79,000 votes, while Clem Shaver, the runner-up, got only 39,000. On national election day he won again, by 70,000 votes, over Republican Senator Henry D. Hatfield. Pathos is added to this picture by the story that the Republicans, having figures that Holt would be easier to beat than Shaver, had thrown some support to the young utility-baiter of Weston, as one of those "clever" campaign tricks which make one despair of the rudimentary intelligence of politicians.

Holt won in spite of the well-advertised fact that he was only twenty-nine years old and would not become thirty until six months after his election, although the Federal Constitution requires that a Senator be thirty years of age. Holt cockily pointed out that Henry Clay had been appointed and seated in the Senate when only twenty-nine, but on the advice of George Norris and Democratic Senatorial leaders, he did not risk a test of his right to sit at the opening of the 1935 session but waited until he should reach the Constitutional age. In the meantime, he established himself in his office and followed the Senate proceedings day by day, while Carter Glass and the other Southern conservatives clawed at the Administration's social policies with a zeal which indicated the depth of the New Deal's challenge to the power of Wall Street.

Holt is primarily a student, who studs his speeches with facts and is not interested in the gas-attack as a method of political warfare. He is a slender, bespectacled, dark-haired youth, a bachelor, whose sister acts as his hostess, and an ardent New Dealer. Progressives of the type of Norris and the LaFollettes are his idols, although he hastened after his election to go to the White House and assure F.D.R. of the falsity of the utility propaganda put out to the effect that he was opposed to the New Deal. He represents a new element in national politics—the post-war generation (he was thirteen when the Armistice came) and the labor reformer from the South. He is not in the least likely to go chasing after a third party candidate in 1936, unless Norris, Costigan and the LaFollettes point the way and unless John L. Lewis and the United Mine Workers give the word. On the other hand, he is not in the least likely to follow the primrose path of election-day liberals and go Wall Street. At the moment, the coal interests and railways in West Virginia form a loose alliance against the hydro-electric and other utilities —for the obvious reason that coal produces freight for the railways and also electric power in steam plants—and Holt is working with them, but in the interest of mine labor and not of bond-holders.

III

West Virginia represents a frontier province for Wall Street, and its resources have been so thoroughly looted that the financiers can contemplate its defection with equanimity. Massachusetts is another story. The breeding nursery, playing-grounds and kindergartens of budding capitalists center in Boston. If Boston and Massachusetts cannot be held safe for capital—in spite of the indiscretion by which New England's good-will was jeopardized through the unloading of Kreuger securities to the Boston intelligentsia (whose attitude was one of quaint consecration: Though Lee Higginson slay me, yet will I praise Morgan)—then capital is lost indeed.

In New England, the most powerful potential leader of a movement toward the "left," with or without Roosevelt, is James Michael Curley, Governor of Massachusetts. So far Curley has stuck to Roosevelt closer than a brother —some brothers are not particularly clubby—and was first on the Roosevelt bandwagon in the pre-convention campaign of 1931–32, and is still on it and playing the key-bugle at that!

Curley is a forceful, ambitious and exceptionally eloquent man. "Back Bay" Boston and the property-owning people of the upper crust of other Massachusetts cities think him capable of anything. They look upon him much as the New Orleans aristocrats look on Huey Long. But such is Massachusetts that the curse of the "better people" has become the equivalent of a guarantee of election. It is among these "better people," rather than in the inner councils of the Democratic Party, that one hears considerable speculation upon the possibility of a Long-Curley or an Olson-Curley ticket in 1936 or 1940. Such speculation fails to do justice to the ebullient successor to "Honey" Fitzgerald: if Curley considers such an alignment, he would probably put himself at the head of the ticket and Long or Olson in second place.

His record in Boston politics has been that of a successful Irish-Catholic politician in the city which, far more than Tammany's New York, is the heaven of Irish-American politicians. He was born in Boston sixty-one years ago, received an education in the local grammar and high schools, entered the traditional political businesses of real estate and insurance and became head of a bank. He entered politics in 1900, by being elected to the Boston Common Council, and from this starting-point his career carried him on up through the Massachusetts House of Representatives, the Boston Board of Aldermen, the Boston City Council, and two terms in Congress (1911–15). Early in his second term, he resigned to become Mayor of Boston, a post in which he served three non-consecutive terms; 1914–18, 1922–26 and 1930–34.

His career in business was as successful as his career in politics, and the atmosphere of prosperity characteristic of municipal political machines which surrounded him and his lieutenants marked him as no fanatic on the subject of clean government. When it is a matter of contracting and real estate deals—as is the general rule in municipal politics—it is easy for reformers to point the finger of scorn but there have been few who have, like Lincoln Steffens, had the courage to point out that respectable banking, big business and especially utilities interests do precisely the same sort of thing and for the identical reason —profit—in State and national politics. The bigger the graft, the harder it is to see. Curley's politics have always been based on the municipal machine, and only now, as Governor, is he entering the larger field of opportunity for the first time.

To become Governor he had to beat one of the most conservative Democratic machines in the country, a machine which was closely identified with the utilities, the manufacturers and mill operators of Massachusetts, who had been at pains to capture both parties for business, just as Wall Street had done in its dealings with Tammany. Curley was serving his third term as Mayor when Roosevelt began to loom up as a powerful candidate for the Democratic Presidential nomination. Governor Joseph B. Ely of Massachusetts was closely allied with Al Smith, Raskob and the Wall Street Democrats, and David I. Walsh, Senior Senator from the Bay State, was trying, as usual, to straddle the fence. Curley sized up the situation as early as 1931, boldly walked into the Roosevelt camp, and burned his bridges behind him in his public utterances. Since he and Ely were bitter enemies, Curley had no other way open to him, if he wished to rise in politics, than to find some other candidate than Al Smith to serve as an autogyro.

Yet Curley was taking a big risk in what he did. Far more than New York, Boston was the most fanatically pro-Smith city in the nation and Curley's following was almost 100 per cent Irish Catholic. Curley himself was

one of the country's leading Catholic laymen—a fact
which helped him and Roosevelt, too—but even after Al
came out openly against F.D.R., Curley held his ground.
He took into political partnership Jimmy Roosevelt, the
President's eldest son, who was also in the insurance business and was hence criticized in holier-than-thou termi-
nology by the "best people" of Boston as though they
hadn't been making millions out of national politics since
their victory in the Civil War, and together Jimmy and
the Mayor made a vigorous fight to elect Roosevelt delegates from Massachusetts. The Smith machine won, two
to one, and Curley had to attend the Chicago Convention
as delegate from the Virgin Islands! However, when
Roosevelt was nominated, Curley had won his gamble
and found himself on top of the heap, with young Jim
beside him.

Naturally he wanted his *quid pro quo.* Some of his
followers took his cue and talked him up as Secretary of
the Interior or Secretary of War, and when the cabinet
was filled without him his next choice was the Ambassadorship to Italy. There were, however, several million
Baptist and Methodist reasons in the Democratic South
why an ardent and conspicuous Catholic should not be
sent to represent the American Government at Rome, and
it was finally arranged that he should be offered the
Ambassadorship to Poland, publicly, so that he could decline it publicly—which he did. The truth was that he
never had intended to go abroad for any length of time—
although he would have liked the Italian assignment for
a short period—since his real objective was the Governorship of Massachusetts, from which Calvin Coolidge had
been catapulted into national politics.

The conservative Democrats led by Ely and Walsh were
in control of the State machine and held a pre-primary

convention in the summer of 1934 which designated General Charles H. Cole as the Democratic nominee for Governor. Cole was a good vote-getter who had come close to being elected in the great Hoover landslide of 1928. Undaunted by the choice of Cole by the convention—a procedure which usually determined the result of the primary—Curley announced himself as an independent candidate for the nomination, running on a liberal New Deal platform. In the primary, Curley, supported by his Boston machine and the fragmentary New Deal machine built up by Jimmy Roosevelt, crushed Cole and the conservative State machine by the overwhelming vote of 284,000 to 128,000. In November, Curley won again by a large margin, although a number of conservative Democrats deserted him, along with the "best people."

His program has been essentially a New Deal program. He has favored organized labor, has supported old age pensions, security and the rest of the current Roosevelt policies, and has favored work relief instead of the dole. He is obviously looking forward to Washington for, despite his sixty years, he is youthful in appearance, a large, heavily-built vigorous man, and in 1936 will probably go after the Senate seat now held by Marcus Coolidge of Fitchburg. No one knows where he will be found if the New Deal starts to wane in the meantime.

One of the most fluent and eloquent orators in the country, Curley is a powerful factor in any political campaign. He is not likely to take a lead in splitting the Democratic party, but if a split occurs, being Boston Irish, he will be found on the side with the best future for James Michael. Whatever the faults of his Boston machine, he has dedicated himself to an essentially liberal program and his routing of the conservative Democrats in 1934 shows the strength of liberalism in Massachusetts quite as much as it does the power of Curley's leadership. The only important qualification to his New Deal loyalty is the fact that he dislikes Roosevelt. He has supported F.D.R. but for some reason the New Deal doesn't seem to have given him all that he desires. Perhaps, like other liberal leaders in conservative constituencies, he will end up by becoming one of the bulwarks of the very interests he has had to fight to achieve power.

IV

Such has been the fate of "The Little Flower" of New York, Fiorello LaGuardia, the Socialist-Republican-Fusionist firebrand who as Mayor of New York has signed on the dotted line indicated by Wall Street.

It was a peculiar combination of circumstances which turned the leading progressive in the House of Representatives into the reform Mayor of the nation's largest city, with the backing of such conservative Republicans as Ogden Mills and Henry Stimson. And it was inevitable, but ironic, that his most conspicuous accomplishment in his first fifteen months as Mayor was to do a perfectly cut-and-dried job of balancing the city's budget, in the course of which he had to apply a sales tax, the very tax that he had prevented Congress from saddling on the nation in 1932.

That is the picture which every Eastern liberal must study so long as Wall Street rules the nation: a thorough-going progressive at the helm of the city of New York, or rather, lashed like Ulysses to the mast and unable to heed the siren call of social reform. For the present, at least, LaGuardia is the main progressive toehold in the East and is a political force to be reckoned with, at least through the campaign of 1936, since his present term as

Mayor does not expire until the end of 1937. Moreover, no politician since Bryan has excelled LaGuardia in the dramatization of popular issues, although his fame spread only gradually beyond the bounds of New York City. He is not a particularly effective speaker, since his manner is jerky, his ideas are apt to splutter, and his voice sometimes cracks into falsetto, but he has plenty of fire and has mastered the trick of making the man in the street—or the subway—understand the issue at stake.

This chunky little Italian-American, with his broad-brimmed soft black hat set on top of his black hair, bushy black eyebrows, black eyes and dusky complexion, is a product of the newer melting-pot—that which took the Slavs, Latins and Jews in millions, where the old melting-pot took the Irish, English and Germans by the hundred thousand—and of the old Western frontier. He is the son of an Italian immigrant who became a bandmaster in the U. S. Army, and grew up in an army post in Arizona. He got a job in the American Consular Service at the age of nineteen and was assigned to Budapest, soon afterwards being shifted to Trieste. From 1904 to 1906 he acted as American Consular Agent at Fiume, where occurred the first of many sensational incidents in his career. In their zeal to have the city of Fiume spick and span for the visit of a Hapsburg Archduchess, the local officials decided that some five hundred unsightly emigrants who were waiting to cross to America in the steerage of a small steamer, ought to be tidied away onto the boat, although it was not to sail for five days. That was the period of Roosevelt's "Perdicaris living or Raisuli dead!" line, and young LaGuardia took his cue from Teddy. "Tell the Archduchess," he said, "that she may boss her own people, but she can't boss the American consul."

Fiorello won that bout and two years later was brought

back to serve as an interpreter at Ellis Island. While serving in that capacity he studied law on the side at New York University and received his law degree in 1910. After five years of none too lucrative private practice, he got a job as State Deputy Attorney-General—this was one of those rare periods when a Fusion Administration ruled the city—and was elected to Congress in 1916. There he remained until 1933, except for one term when he served as President of the Board of Aldermen of New York, back in 1920.

When America entered the World War, LaGuardia learned to fly at Mineola and then took a contingent of 150 American aviation cadets to Europe, the first one to be sent over. On reaching the Continent he was hustled off as morale-builder to his ancestral Italy, which was staggering under the blow of Caporetto, and was put in command of the aviation school at Fioggia and of the American air forces on the Italian front, where he did plenty of flying against the Austrians over the most corrugated terrain known to war-aviators. His main job, however, was to cheer up the Italian will to resistance by telling them that the Yanks were coming, and he did so with great effect, speaking to capacity crowds in the principal cities of Italy.

His cadets adored him and his zeal and impatience led him to tear the sacred Army regulations into shreds in order to get results. He was once summoned to France and threatened with court-martial for buying food for his men from Italian hotels instead of from the nearest American quartermaster in France. LaGuardia replied that there was no way to get the rations shipped from France to Italy and that his men had to be fed, even if it wasn't military to feed them by unorthodox methods. That just made his offense worse and he was told that he would be court-martialed. He replied to his superiors that they had better read the first article of the Army regulations, which says that the Secretary of War shall make all Army regulations. He added that if the regulations didn't cover his case, he would go back to Washington and get some regulations made which would. At this moment his superiors suddenly remembered that he was in Congress as well as in uniform and decided not to bother about the court-martial.

LaGuardia's Congressional history at one time was regarded as being as scandalous and in as bad taste as the Kingfish's subsequent career. Barney Baruch in particular was depressed by LaGuardia's failure to realize the advantages of the sales tax. However, in those days the Little Flower was able to indulge his progressive principles to the full. Here are some of the things he did in his Congressional career:

Fought the high cost of living, in the period right after the War.

Fought high coal prices.

Forced one Federal judge to resign under threat of impeachment and had two others censured by the House Judiciary Committee.

Joined Senator Shipstead in introducing the first anti-injunction bill for the protection of labor and later, working with Senator Norris, saw it become law.

Launched the campaign for a Congressional investigation of the administration of the bankruptcy laws and saw his charges substantiated by the investigation.

Opposed the Espionage Act during the War.

Sponsored the 30-year retirement program for Federal employees, now in effect.

Introduced the first post-war resolutions for disarmament and the renunciation of war as a national policy.

Was the leading opponent of the "Power Trust" in the House.

During his first term in Congress, was the first to urge Congress to congratulate the Russian people on the overthrow of the Romanoffs.

Proposed the death penalty for war-profiteers.

Prophesied that the war-loans to the Allies would not be repaid to any substantial amount and proposed instead, at the time they were authorized, that the money be advanced as a gift rather than a loan.

Blocked the Baker plan for a large standing army immediately after the War.

Led the fight for repeal of the Espionage Act.

Dramatized the fight against the Volstead Law, once by mixing a malt tonic and near beer to make a 2 per cent alcoholic beverage which he served openly in his office and on New York street corners, defying the Federal authorities to prosecute him.

Blocked the national sales tax in 1932, when the Democrats, under the orders of Raskob, Baruch, Hearst and similar leaders, combined with the conservative Republicans to put it over, and forced the substitution of higher income taxes for this tax on necessities.

Advocated old age pensions, unemployment insurance, a big public works program and so on.

In fact, a complete list of LaGuardia's exploits in Congress would require an eight-page pamphlet and probably will, but he succeeded in combining sensationalism with consistent liberalism, a penetrating mind, extraordinary thoroughness, and complete you-be-damned courage. As a result, the conservatives were constantly gunning for him inside and out of the machine, and to stay in Congress he ran variously as a Republican, a

Progressive, and an Independent with Socialist endorsement. He was also somewhat aided by the fact that his election workers included some of the most proficient Italian knife and knuckle men ever assembled in New York politics. He left the Republicans in 1924 to support LaFollette and Wheeler and frequently supported individual Democrats. Twice the Republicans solemnly in Congress read him out of the party and deprived him of his committee appointments but they never made a dent on his influence, and he was constantly compelling them to seek his aid.

In 1929, with characteristic insolence, the Little Flower went out and won the Republican nomination for Mayor of New York, to the disgust of the "silk-stocking" Republicans. He made a savage campaign against Jimmy Walker, making many charges against him which were later substantiated by the Tuttle and Seabury investigations, but was overwhelmingly beaten by Tammany. It was in this campaign that so many of the wealthy Republicans voted for Norman Thomas ("who is at least a gentleman") instead of for this Italian-American "radical" freebooter. Four years later, LaGuardia went unabashed and got the nomination again. At the eleventh hour, the Farley-Flynn combination tried to beat him and smash Tammany at the same time by trotting out poor Holy Joe McKee on a new-laid "Recovery Party" ticket. Fiorello won anyhow.

It was a great blow to all concerned. The firebrand has had to content himself with the palliative politics of self-accusing social systems: clean government, efficient government, balance-the-budget government. The financial difficulties that he inherited from Tammany prevented his adopting the progressive type of program he might

have tried in better times, but he made some liberal appointments, packed the statue of Civic Virtue off to Brook-
lyn, made a big play against Hitler's treatment of the Jews
(LaGuardia has Jewish blood, and thirty per cent of his
electorate is Jewish), and, with the aid of Federal money,
pushed ahead with slum clearance, park programs and
other by-products of the stymied social conscience.

To do this he has established friendly relations with
the New Deal and Adolf A. Berle, Jr., one of the charter-
members of the original Roosevelt Brain Trust, has been
with him from the start of his campaign. The close collaboration between the White House and the Little
Flower, especially in the effort to drive down utility rates
in New York City, has caused regurgitations in the financial district and some quick fixing at Albany. During the
1934 campaign, LaGuardia went to Wisconsin and spoke
for the two LaFollettes. His frequent outbursts irritate the
conservative Republicans who helped make him Mayor
but they dare not turn against him yet, as he balanced
the budget and cleaned up some of the worst of the local
messes, and he may be useful in 1936.

While his political future may lie in any one of a large
number of directions—not excluding the Fascistic—his
natural affiliation is with the LaFollettes. If they stick
with the New Deal, he is likely to do so, although he
might go down the line for a reasonably progressive Republican. He is not likely to line up with the Kingfish,
as his own understanding of economic and social problems is too mature to permit him to swallow the decep-
tive simplicity and demagogic lack of substance of the
"Share-Our-Wealth" program. It is unlikely that he will
be reëlected Mayor in 1937—as New York gets tired of reform very easily and the Democrats are naturally in the
overwhelming majority—and so the Little Flower will

lack assets for 1940, unless he utilizes 1936 as a spring-
board. Where he really ought to be is in the U. S. Senate,
as a running-mate for Bob Wagner.

Yet despite all of his fire and fervor and progressivism,
there is something inherently unsubstantial about La-
Guardia as about all of the Eastern "radicals." The measure of their "radicalism" is the fact that the LaFollette
influence is about as far "left" as the Eastern wild men
will dare to go, and the LaFollettes are pretty far to the
"right" in terms of Western sentiment. So long as other
things are equal—by which is meant the continuance of
the system by which big business and high finance run
the nation's affairs from Wall Street—there may be
alarums and excursions and barrages and raids on the
Eastern front, but the end of all such rebellions is frustration and further subjugation. The only chance of real
change is the possibility that the liberal forces of the West
and South, working together with such doubtful allies
in the Northeast, may alter the rules of the game before
Wall Street recovers its balance. But there are plenty of
shrewd, colorful and ruthless men in the field who are
determined to prevent this from ever happening and it
is, in fact, their efforts to break up the liberal coalition
(as they have succeeded in doing on several previous occasions) which is the cause of the sudden appearance of
the "lunatic fringe" in national politics.

XII

RALLY-ROUND-THE-FLAG BOYS

THE APPEARANCE of mad-dog demagogues and Tory mud-slingers under the New Deal is nothing new in America. What is new is the fact that the cat-calls and short, ugly words of the wave of agitation which broke in the early spring of 1935 bears an alarmingly close relationship to political realities. It is the reality that is shocking, rather than the epithet. There is a surging current of resentment under the formerly smooth surface of American life, which has swirled to the top in seething eddies of anger, frustration and despair. At the same time, the surface itself is congealing into a frozen lid, designed to hold down the force of realities and keep them from expressing themselves in practical affairs.

For seventy years, the character of American political institutions has been based on grotesque unrealities. The Civil War smashed the traditional pattern of our life, as a democracy, composed chiefly of farmers and planters, in which the only permanent class-distinctions were based on color and previous condition of servitude. The Republican Revolution of the 1860's destroyed not only Jeffersonian simplicity but also Jacksonian democracy and left the American people struggling in a maze of false issues against an army of political ghosts.

The fruits of the Civil War and of the Republican Revolution which it achieved are simple. It created and established a permanent Union around a strong central government at a terrible cost. Part of this cost took the

form of a political system based on two sectional parties
which ignored geography and economics and which established a Solid North of manufacturers, miners, merchants,
bankers and farmers as opposed to a Solid South of former
slave-owning farmers, instead of the natural division between the agricultural West and the Eastern business,
banking and manufacturing interests. The "Bloody Shirt"
and the "Lost Cause" were substituted for political
thought, for three blasted generations.

The economic cost was still greater. As a result of this
weird political set-up, the American System was able to
take its painfully familiar form of a business empire
operating autocratically within—and by the aid of—a
political democracy. The empire which American business created on the basis of the Union, plus the Fourteenth
Amendment, has ruled ruthlessly ever since and has held
itself immune from the normal processes of politics.
America became the only great nation in which the government could not control business. Business was a State
within the State, a law unto itself, a world lacking checks
and balances and a sense of obligation to or responsibility
for the social welfare. Great bankers like the Elder J. P.
Morgan, great railway manipulators like the late E. H.
Harriman, great industrialists like Andrew Carnegie,
Henry Ford and John D. Rockefeller, dealt with the political government and with Presidents, as with their
equals if not their vassals. The courts became their allies
in this process so completely that even today we find a
Federal Judge ruling that it is "confiscatory" for the Federal Government to produce hydro-electric energy for
sale to the people of the Tennessee Valley.

The social cost of the Civil War, which grew out of this
process of economic imperialism based on the political
conquest of the South by the North, proved unbearably

high, as was evidenced by constant rebellions and a decline of the birth rate which could be concealed only by the constant importation of fresh peasant stock from Europe. The social cost took the form of subduing both industrial laborers and freehold farmers to the position of economic subjects in the business empire. Despite sentimental enactments, labor became and has remained a commodity. At the same time farm production became simply part of industrial raw materials. Credit became the essential element in economic exchange and in a nation which lives by credit the money-lender is king. Out of this process emerged a landless mass of city slum-dwellers whose only claim on production was the opportunity to hire themselves as labor to the employers, and a bankrupt and precarious farm tenantry who rapidly constituted a rural slum-life as deplorable as that of our worst cities.

While American politics were still conducted on the theory that we had a representative government, under democracy, with equality of opportunity and no permanent distinctions, the real life of the nation was conducted according to the facts: that business, by which we live, is an autocracy, in which the object as among competitors is to prevent equality of opportunity and of which the result has been the production of a population, nine-tenths of which is under-privileged and one-third of which is economically disenfranchised.

This economic autocracy was superimposed suddenly and by brute force on a nation which was not prepared for it. The result has been a constant rumble of unrest, punctuated by panics, by hard times and by wars, and productive of three great rebellions against the business empire which was being built up inside the old structure of representative democracy. And correspondingly, the business

rulers have developed a technique—based largely on patri-
otism and Constitutional ancestor-worship—for subduing
revolt.

The first of these rebellions arose and petered out in
the 1870's and 1880's—the period when the Trusts appeared, headed by Standard Oil and the railways, and directed by the Neanderthalers of American business—Jim
Fisk, Jay Gould, Daniel Drew and the elder Rockefeller.
This "peasants' revolt" was easily crushed. When the
pinch came President Cleveland ordered out the Federal
troops to break the Pullman strike, the money power was
handed over to the private bankers, and the first Anti-
Trust Law was used, with amazing skill, as the basis for
judicial injunctions against labor unions as "combina-
tions in restraint of trade."

The second rebellion followed shortly thereafter. The
Populists and the Greenbackers joined with the Democrats in a mighty struggle to elect William Jennings Bryan
on a platform which, by proposing the free and unlimited
coinage of silver money, was a direct challenge to the auto-
cratic powers of the gold bankers of New York. It was felt
that the Government should free itself from a system
which made it dependent upon private money-lenders.

There was a short, sharp campaign, based on wild emotionalism, in which propagandists like "Coin" Harvey
and the predecessors of the "Bonus Marchers"—Coxey's
Army—played their part in whipping up enthusiasm for
Bryan, while the business magnates, led by Mark Hanna
of Ohio, employed intimidation and corruption on a wide
scale. Bryan was defeated and the "New York Tribune"
exulted over his defeat in terms which anticipated General
Hugh Johnson by nearly thirty years:

. . . the wretched rattle-pated boy (Bryan), posing in vapid
vanity and mouthing resounding rottenness, was not the real

leader of that league of hell. He was only a puppet in the
blood-imbued hands of Altgeld, the anarchist, and Debs, the
revolutionist, and other desperadoes of that stripe. But he
was a willing puppet, Bryan was—willing and eager. None of
his masters was more apt than he at lies and forgeries and
blasphemies and all the nameless iniquities of that campaign
against the Ten Commandments.

The third rebellion came not long after American business, led by Hearst and Pulitzer, tried to short-circuit
"domestic unrest" by the War with Spain and the so-
called Full Dinner Pail. This War, while adding the
Philippines and Cuba to our national headaches, gave
national fame to a young New York politician named
Theodore Roosevelt, who led a charge up San Juan Hill
and was elected Governor of his State in consequence.
Roosevelt was "unsound"—he had ideas—and was quietly
put into the lethal chamber reserved for embarrassing
politicians—the Vice-Presidency. Then President McKin-
ley was assassinated and Roosevelt the First inaugurated
an era of Trust-Busting, political pyrotechnics and reform
which came to an end only when Woodrow Wilson was
jockeyed into the World War in 1917.

For, just about the time when Wilson was threatening
to bring about a real reform, the World War impelled
him to abandon domestic matters and go crusading for
democracy in Europe. By the time the War ended and he
was ready to return to the job he had neglected at home
it was too late. He was hounded out of office as mercilessly
as any man in our history and the third rebellion had
failed. Instead, we got Harding and normalcy and a confused impression that the nutrition of Esthonian and
Belgian babies and the financial rehabilitation of France
were more important to us, as a people, than the welfare
of our own children and our individual solvency.

One last desperate rear-guard action was fought by LaFollette in 1924, but the result was a foregone conclusion. He was crushed, and his defeat discredited for eight years the expectation that reform could be achieved by ordinary political methods.

There remained the possibility of revolution.

This possibility was ignored for the eight fateful years in which America lived under a financial army of occupation, while bond-salesmen and stock-brokers and bankers ruled the land in the name of Mammon, the Merciful, the Compassionate.

The first four years and all was well. Coolidge sat in the White House and the "Sons of the Wild Jackass," the statesmen from the American Steppes, led by George Norris of Nebraska, with occasional allocutions from Borah of Idaho, remained as the voices crying in the wilderness, but voices were all they were. American organized labor had decided that the fear of Bolshevism was the beginning of high wages and the physical task of reconstructing Europe, with American money and material, provided work for nearly everyone.

Then came Hoover. With Hoover came the Panic. After the Panic came the Depression. For three dreadful years Hoover stuck to his guns and refused to admit the need or desirability for any material change in our political, business or social system. This do-nothing policy stunned the country into a mood of despair so profound that it has never fully recovered its morale. There was a slow fermentation and a process of incubation, here and there throughout the nation. Communists played up the prevailing distress, but made few converts. Penny auctions and anti-eviction riots testified to the tearing up of the social contract by masses of our people but it was all without form, without theory, without leadership, without an aim. It resembled nothing so much as the reflex contortions of a man under an anaesthetic.

By 1932, however, the situation had become so desperate that fresh leadership, at any cost, was necessary. By the early summer, small independent political groups were forming in every part of the country. Over two hundred of them came into existence and continued to function for about a year. The charming unreality of American politics was suddenly invaded by a swarm of confused and clamorous groups demanding action and a new political line-up. In addition to a growing respect for Communism and Socialism, the examples of Italy, Russia, and Japan and the growth of the Nazi movement in Germany, as well as the formation of the National Government in England, suggested that a great nation could alter its political mechanisms and its social and business forms without catastrophe. It seemed finally that the only choice was between radical revolution and Rooseveltian reform.

The Democratic Party, largely against its will and certainly against the desires of its financial backers, was compelled by this movement to adopt a liberal candidate who would be independent of Big Business. The liberals and progressives and the vociferous spokesmen of the lunatic fringe nominated Franklin Roosevelt with acclamation, amid the shocked head-shaking of conservatives and big business men, and elected him on a platform of reform.

II

By this time, however, the conservatives had become adept in the art of sowing the whirlwind and reaping the shorn lamb, and they proceeded on the theory that Roosevelt's talk of reform was "for the record" but that his real purpose would be "recovery," which meant, according to Tory doctrine, the restoration of the same old profits to the same old profiteers. Impossible though such a program was of realization—for the only way you could save the racket was by letting the individual racketeers take their chance of bankruptcy—there were plenty of men who believed it not only possible but highly desirable. The accidental agent in their effort to establish a system of recovery in which there should be no losses, just profits, was General Hugh Johnson of the Blue Eagle and the N.R.A.

By now, everybody has heard of Hugh Johnson, even if he is sometimes confused with Hiram Johnson on the other side of the Atlantic. His antics in N.R.A., his "cracking-down," his lurid vocabulary, Gargantuan energy and formidable pugnacity, marked him as a man who could do the impossible. Yet now that it is all over and the attempt to secure recovery without reform has been abandoned, we are still left with a sense of wonder.

How did he get that way? Where does he go from here? What did he mean? He meant that American business was given a chance to reform itself, on a guarantee that it would produce recovery, and muffed the chance, despite the utmost conceivable energy and good-will on the part of the chosen leader for National Industrial Recovery. Even a genius could not do the trick, for it is not a mistake to call Johnson a "genius," as Ray Moley did.

His mixture of energy, mental agility, boundless ambition, versatility, literary skill and supercharged emotionalism fits into no other category. The person most like him in our public life is Huey Long, and Long is narrower, less well-educated, and unable to zoom into the patriotic stratosphere in which Hugh Johnson moves, in all sincerity. Yet the more you look at Hugh and Huey the more they look like psychological twins, which is an-other reason for going light on entrusting national power to the Mussolini of Baton Rouge. We've tried a benevo-lent and pro-business dictator, and had to discard him in the interest of national progress.

The demise of Johnson as the "Big Man" of the New Deal—next to F.D.R.—is an American Tragedy, accord-ing to Johnson's "The Blue Eagle from Egg to Earth," but it was a plain necessity to the New Deal, for which Johnson had become the greatest handicap. The fault was not so much Johnson's as it was the law and theory behind the recovery program. The idea of establishing minimum wages and limitation of hours was economically and socially sound, but when the Chamber of Commerce boys—the big business leaders who were on their knees in sackcloth and ashes—were invited to take a crack at the Thirty-Hour Week Bill of 1933 and converted it into the National Industrial Recovery Act, the result was bound to be what the result had always been before—monopoly and profiteering, without compensation to the public. Wages and hours of employment should have been imposed on industry, but as the law was contrived, the wage and hour reforms were turned into grudging concessions that business made in return for all that it could get in the way of devices to outlaw competition, safeguard existing investments, and guarantee increased profits. Johnson's "cracking-down" was just empty show-manship. It annoyed a lot of business men but they got what they wanted, as Johnson was hopelessly out-traded —although he never realized it and apparently doesn't yet.

The next move was equally obvious—to all save the General. N.R.A.'s interference with little business created a backfire; N.R.A. made exceptions, retreats and modifications to satisfy the little fellows; the net result was that big business, having acquired monopoly, began to shake free of its concessions to labor. By the summer of 1934, the idea that the N.R.A. was bearing down on the little fellow was about 90 per cent bunk, although it was true of a few codes and there were troublesome wage differentials between cities and rural districts, and between different regions.

What the N.R.A. did, on the whole, was to try to freeze the status quo. It became an instrument of monopoly—not through giving established big units an advantage but by giving competitive industries the same opportunity to exploit the public that the monopolies had. The N.R.A. did some good, without question, but the New Deal propaganda that it was primarily responsible for recovery in the first two years of the Roosevelt Administration, will not stand analysis. Far more important was the restoration of agricultural purchasing power, through abandoning the gold standard, through refinancing farm debts at lower rates, and through the A.A.A.

In fact, the N.R.A. tended to hold back the real motive power of recovery—the capital goods industries; it hiked the price of lumber and other building materials; it threw safeguards around existing capital structures which needed to be put through the wringer; and generally discouraged technological improvements and expansion. Under Johnson, it was a protective device for existing capital and for its managers, rather than a stimulus to recovery.

The curious thing about Johnson's apology for N.R.A. is that he boasts that every code was agreed to by business and asserts that he bulldozed no code committee. He swears that he held an even hand, rapping business when it needed it, rapping labor when it asked too much. What he does not boast about is the fact that he did his best, and successfully, to squelch and discredit all the economists who were trying to tell him what would be the result of the policies he was adopting: a shriveling up of buying power, leading to fresh depression—as actually occurred in the autumn of 1934.

Yet Johnson is not dumb. He was highly qualified by his knowledge of the American business and industrial set-up—acquired as research man for Barney Baruch—and he had done a lot of thinking and, with his army and war experience, his thinking was in terms of the national interest. His doctrine, like that of Henry Wallace and Rex Tugwell, was "balance" and, with George N. Peek, he had been one of the originators of the equalization fee scheme to rescue agriculture from the post-war depression. But Johnson could never get away from the business man's or investor's point of view on fundamentals: that the loss could always be passed on to the other fellow. He saw no absurdity in the establishment of industrial codes which, in the aggregate, proposed to charge the public far more than the aggregate purchasing power that the codes released.

No man could have undertaken such a task without taking a bad beating. Even as N.I.R.A. was written, however, it could have been directed along different lines, concentrating on the big industries, imposing wage and hour restrictions, avoiding the emotional ballyhoo of the Blue Eagle. By the late autumn of 1933, notwithstanding the General's showmanship, there was considerable appreciation high up on the inside of the New Deal that the N.R.A. was going sour and that nothing much could be done about it except under fresh leadership. However, Johnson was under such fire, with threats of investigations, that he couldn't quit gracefully and the President would not permit him to do so under external pressure. From the first of 1934, one of the major problems of the New Deal was how to ease Johnson out of the N.R.A. and redirect it into smoother channels.

Johnson was the soul of loyalty to Roosevelt and was dedicated to the success of the New Deal, *as he conceived it,* but could not conceive its succeeding without his, Johnson's, particular policy. He saw a lot of his mistakes and recast his policy in many directions but he was still obsessed with the idea of putting everybody under a code. It was a sort of Selective Service Act for industry. His idea was to draft everybody and then begin to break them in and weed them out, through industrial training camps. This policy seriously miscalculated the public psychology. Finally, Johnson, fighting furiously to hold his ground, completely lost his perspective.

His plan for the badly battered Blue Eagle was to stage another Blue Eagle drive in the spring of 1934. It was stymied by Frank Walker, Director of the National Emergency Council, with the approval of the White House. Johnson, whirling like a dervish, fighting on all fronts, erupting crackling epithets, was in such a high-pitched emotional state that he didn't realize that the country had long since ceased to respond to the fervor of the summer of 1933. In his book he gives the impression that the Blue Eagle failed to hatch its chickens because of sabotage within the Administration and he attributes his own slide down the bannisters to Donald Richberg and Madam Secretary Perkins.

The truth is that Johnson simply couldn't take a hint and he thought—or seemed to think—that all major movements in the Administration originated in the N.R.A. Yet Richberg did not desert him or stir up rebellion against him. On the contrary, Richberg himself was sus-

pected of being too closely attached to the Johnson policies. After it had been decided that among all the people
who knew the inside of N.R.A. he was the best qualified
to do the job of salvage, Richberg was simply weaned
away from Johnson by unseen but well-directed hands.

Roosevelt, who hates being frank with his friends, made
several efforts to ease Johnson out in a graceful manner.
Johnson himself tells of the President's proposal that he
go abroad to study European recovery methods, and how
the President urged him to take a vacation. But Johnson
was still fighting to hang on and the President didn't want
him to resign in a huff: in fact on at least two occasions
he dissuaded Johnson from resigning at all. How to force
a big man out of a big job and make him like it is, indeed,
a difficult problem. Roosevelt finally solved the problem
last autumn. Bernard M. Baruch went to Hyde Park at
the President's invitation one fine September day, and
shortly afterward Johnson submitted his resignation and
got a friendly acceptance from the President.

However, the idea that Johnson was a "tool" of Baruch
as head of the N.R.A. is so much horsefeathers. He is
intensely loyal to Baruch, under whom he worked on the
War Industries Board and with whom he was intimately
associated in business for many years. His thinking was
also greatly influenced by Baruch's ideas, who has one
of the subtlest and most philosophical intellects in the
business world. Yet Baruch frequently, if rather pater-
nally, complained that Hugh, as head of the N.R.A., never
consulted him. If he had, Baruch's far cooler head might
have saved Johnson some of his worst blunders.

Johnson and Roosevelt are great admirers of each other.
F.D.R. was—and still is—extremely fond of Hugh, and
undoubtedly would like to use the amazing Johnsonian
talents, though it is hard to pick a job which requires

them in a process of reconstruction and reform. The Senate would be a better place than the Administration for Johnson, and the latter's idea that he might get into the Senate by going back to his old State of Oklahoma and beating Gore in 1936 has received some encouragement in New Deal quarters, especially since Gore has voted against the Administration on several important issues.

However, Johnson's attack on Coughlin and Long was his own idea. As a publicity stunt to help sell his book and launch his newspaper column, it was superb. As politics, it made a lot of wise New Deal managers pretty sick. Although they enjoyed it tremendously in private, they felt it would help Long and Coughlin more than it hurt them. In retrospect, however, it was too big an indiscretion to be a blunder. It supplied Long with an opportunity to broadcast his "Share-Our-Wealth" policy, thus marking a distinct turning-point in the Kingfish's progress, while it had the effect of making Coughlin reassert his faith in Roosevelt. That reassertion would have come sooner or later anyhow—or at least Coughlin probably couldn't have teamed up with Long in a very active way without running afoul of the Church—but it accelerated the separation of the two spokesmen of ultra-New Deal economics and contributed to the clearing of the atmosphere.

Johnson is not the sort of man who is likely to sink completely out of sight. His pen is too biting; his sense of publicity values is too strong; he is, moreover, an extremely valuable man. Despite his essentially conservative outlook, he is too unpredictable, too dramatic, too highly emotional to make a "safe" man for big business and finance to follow. And he has written, "Any human economic and political system has failed when people can no longer live under it by their own efforts." This is heresy when set against the business theory that it is not the sys-

velt, by trying to get States to send uninstructed or "favorite son" delegations to the National Convention. The Roosevelt people beat him time and again, in one Southern and Midwestern State after another, but an anti-Roosevelt coalition was formed which was strong enough to bar Roosevelt from the two-thirds majority needed to nominate without some trading in the convention.

In the spring of 1932 there was a memorable meeting of the Convention Committee in Chicago. Shouse wanted to be the "keynoter" and he could plead that his three years of work for the Party entitled him to this recognition, but the Roosevelt people couldn't afford to let the representative of Raskob and Smith—the "Stop-Roosevelt" gang—sound the convention keynote. They balked and insisted on Barkley of Kentucky for the job. Shouse had many personal friends among the Roosevelt representatives at the meeting and some of them had committed themselves to Shouse so far as the keynote was concerned. There were some hurried calls from them to Roosevelt and Howe—and Shouse was told that Roosevelt agreed that he could be the Permanent Chairman of the Convention, if Barkley made the keynote speech. (Harry F. Byrd, who even then nursed Presidential ambitions, negotiated this deal.) The Roosevelt people deny that they made any commitment and soon afterward they held a conference at Hyde Park, and announced that Walsh of Montana would be their candidate for permanent chairman. Obviously they could not afford to have an enemy in such an important position, where the power to recognize or to refuse to recognize and to make rulings, may, in a close fight, mean the difference between the Presidential nomination and being an also-ran.

This fight over the permanent chairmanship was the first big fight of the convention. The Roosevelt people won. Shouse, embittered, was out of the picture; and, with the nomination of Roosevelt, he was out of his job on the National Committee, along with his backer Raskob. The latter and his close friend, Pierre S. DuPont, had another "baby"—the Association Against the Prohibition Amendment (there being an innocent belief that the imposition of liquor taxes would prevent higher income taxes). Shouse took over the presidency of this organization and carried it through until the repeal of the Eighteenth Amendment in December, 1933. That left him without a job. He has a law office in Washington but he no longer had that prestige which goes with being the president or chairman of an organization that gets in the news.

In August, 1934, after several months of preliminary wrangling, this deficiency was made good, and Mr. Shouse who, with Herbert Hoover, was becoming concerned over the possibility that reform might interfere with existing arrangements and personnel in the upper reaches of business, announced the decision to form the American Liberty League. Its chief backers were: John W. Davis (attorney for J. P. Morgan & Co.), Nathan L. Miller (Counsel for the U. S. Steel Corporation), Irenée DuPont (munitions), Representative James W. Wadsworth, Jr. (old-fashioned Tory Republican), Alfred E. Smith (the forgotten man), and John J. Raskob (ex-General Motors). Probably no organization was ever launched more ineptly or with less auspicious sponsorship, given the state of public opinion. All of the most vulnerable political targets in the country were compressed into one bull's-eye.

Mr. Shouse said that the League was not against Roosevelt and wasn't anti-New Deal, but Mr. Roosevelt apparently thought otherwise. Two days later in his press conference, he praised the League with faint damns, by endorsing its avowed aim to defend the Constitution but

EUGENE TALMADG[E]

HUEY LONG

UPTON SINCLAIR

MILO RENO

DR. FRANCIS E. TOWNSEN[D]

BIBB GRAVES

PHILIP LA FOLLETTE